The Awesome Power of Positive Attention

THE AWESOME POWER OF
POSITIVE
ATTENTION

JOHN W. DRAKEFORD

BROADMAN PRESS
NASHVILLE, TENNESSEE

Unless otherwise noted, all Scripture notations are taken from the *King James Version* of the Bible.

All Scripture notations marked (NIV) are from the Holy Bible, *New International Version*, copyright © 1973, 1978, 1984 by International Bible Society.

Library of Congress Cataloging-in-Publication Data

Drakeford, John W.
    The awesome power of positive attention / John W. Drakeford.
        p.   cm.
    ISBN 0-8054-6030-6
    1. Interpersonal communication. 2. Attention-seeking.   I. Title.
BF637.C45D85 1991
153.6--dc20
                                                                90-39929
                                                                    CIP

To Eve
Robina's youngest sister, a beautiful dreamer,
who became a most attentive mother and grandmother

Preface

"I am a direct descendant from Fletcher Christian who led the mutineers in the mutiny on the Bounty," boasted Naomi, a Pitcairn Islander. She was evidence of Queen Victoria's policy of providing a place for descendants of the Bounty mutineers to live. They had taken refuge on Pitcairn Island, but soon there was not enough room for the expanding population. The queen then gave them permission to take over the former penal colony of Norfolk Island. Most of the islanders moved to their new home and remained there.

Norfolk Island must be one of the most beautiful spots in the world and is frequently called "The Pacific Island Paradise." However, in its early days it was settled by the British as a penal settlement, and the most incorrigible convicts were sent to this five-by-three-mile island for punishment. It became known by names like "The Isle of Misery," "The Hell Hole of the Pacific," and the similar names.

On March 6, 1840, the ship *Nautilus* arrived at Norfolk Island with a notable passenger, Captain Alexander Maconochie, who had come to run the infamous penal settlement. From Maconochie's previous experience he had learned the futility of using force. He came to Norfolk Island with the original idea about how the penal colony should be run.

Maconochie described the condition of the 1,400 prisoners on Norfolk Island, "In every way their feelings were habitually outraged, and their self-respect destroyed. For the 'merest trifles' the convicts were flogged, ironed, or confined for days on bread and water. They were fed more like hogs than men."[1] This treatment had resulted in embittered, recalcitrant prisoners who became more intractable as time went on.

Maconochie's proposal was that the emphasis should be on reform rather than punishment. He proposed this idea be carried out by giving the convicts positive focused attention through his mark system. He inaugurated the concept that "The fate of every man should be placed unreservedly in his own hands."[2] An overseer of marks was appointed. For each good behavior there was an allotment of marks and for each bad behavior a debit of marks. It was possible through the mark system for a diligent convict to earn enough marks to cut his sentence in half.

The act of entering the marks was itself an indication of attention to these people who felt they were completely without hope.

The fruits of the program were seen in a landmark event that took place on Norfolk Island in celebration of the late Queen Victoria's birthday on May 25, 1840. The gates of prison were thrown open, and distinctions between guards and prisoners were forgotten for the day. All spent a memorable day mixing and mingling and attending theatrical performances presented by the convicts who showed themselves to have unusual dramatic ability during the event. Guards and prisoners sat and ate dinner together.

Since the traditional purpose of the penal system was punishment, Maconochie's immediate superior, Sir George Gibbs, wrote to his superior Lord John Russel, complaining about the "crimes" in handling the convicts. Russel in response gave instructions that Maconochie should be sent to another post, and Norfolk Island went back to being the Isle of Despair.

All of this might well be a parable of life. There are certain skills of behavior alteration that could introduce many tremendous changes in people's lives. At the heart of these are wide ranges of using attention. This is the focus of this book. My aim will be to teach people about attention: especially what to do when they can't get it and don't know how to give it. Keep that in mind as you read this book.

Notes

1. Frank Clune, *The Norfolk Island Story* (Sydney: Angus and Robertson, 1981), 190-91.

2. Robert Hughes, *The Fatal Shore*, (London: Collins Harvil, 1987), 500.

Contents

Part 1:

The Desperate Search
for Attention

1

Recognizing Attention Starvation

*"What people want is a little attention
as human beings."*
—William Lyon Phelps

As it bumped along the road, the jeep brought a welcome movement of the humid tropical air through the lush vegetation with its squawking birds, and after several hours of teeth-rattling driving, finally arriving at the small grass hut. This humble dwelling was the temporary home of a Dutch missionary family recently released from a World War II prisoner of war camp. They extended an overwhelming welcome, and we were soon enjoying a happy, prolonged conversation. The time flew, and as the clock approached noon, I reluctantly announced I would need to leave for my camp. The whole family—father, mother, and two children—pleaded with me to stay for lunch, assuring me that they had plenty of food.

The Australian Army had strange ideas about what food the troops should eat. Apparently, sheep tired of living were periodically eaten. Vegetables of uncertain age were prepared, and the end result was a concoction called M&V—meat and vegetables.

You can imagine my horror as I sat at the Bott table to discover that the Australian Army also supplied their rations. The meal was to be M&V. I tried to think up some way out of my difficulty. I *could* suddenly get sick and not be able to eat, or I *could* remember an appointment, which would mean getting back to camp immediately.

While I mentally mulled over the situation, Mrs. Bott asked her daughter Wilhelmina to ask God's blessings on the food. We bowed our heads, and the little girl rattled off the words of the blessing in Dutch. When I asked the mother to interpret for me, Mrs. Bott repeated, "Thank you, God, for this delicious food."

I leaned over to the little girl and said, "Wilhelmina, this is not delicious food."

Mrs. Bott interrupted, "It might not be delicious to you, Chaplain, but a little girl who has lived for years in a prisoner of war camp on the edge of starvation finds it delicious."

Wilhelmina was an example of people who have suffered the rigors of starvation because of war; others have been put through the experience because of drought; still others by the destruction of crops by diseases and pests; and yet others by the devastation of great natural disturbances like earthquakes and floods.

The Agony of Famine

All of the foregoing factors have created the torment of famine which has periodically swept across the world. Probably the earliest example of famine was in Egypt where Joseph, following his dream about the lean and fat cows, warned the pharaoh and set up a plan for coping with the disaster. In the fourteenth century the Great Famine of Bengal (a province of India) claimed the lives of one third of the population. Later in 1790, in that same country came the Skull Famine, so called because the dead were too numerous to bury. In Ireland the potato famine came from the failure of that staple food, and in

England a famine in 1586 gave rise to the Poor Law system.

However, famines did not just happen in the ancient past. In the ten-year period of 1940-50, famine stalked Europe in the ghettos of Warsaw, the prison camps in Central Europe, the Netherlands, Greece, and besieged Leningrad. The tragedy has moved on, in later days, in such places as Africa, Asia, and and other nations. Starvation is a specter that periodically haunts the bodies and minds of vast numbers of people.

Like the bread that people desperately need, if they are to survive, there is a psychological need of the human personality that must be satisfied, if people are to discover their potential. It is called the *hunger for attention.*

"Man shall not live by bread alone unless there is no bread," is the statement sometimes used to introduce the highly respected, motivational theory of needs developed by Abraham Maslow. Maslow postulates that humans have a succession of needs commencing with physiological needs (bread) following the satisfaction of which safety needs become obvious, followed in turn by esteem needs, and then self-actualizing needs, the latter being at the peak of the hierarchy. Probably Maslow's most significant service was to show that no sooner had one need been satisfied than another emerged, making a human in his words "a perpetually wanting animal."

Attention-Seeking Individual

There is an important implication in Maslow's theory: namely that *a person is an attention-seeking individual.* At the physiological level, the provision of food, drink, and shelter gives the subject the sense of the attention of parents or guardians. Safety needs being satisfied bring the message of ever-present caregivers. The provision of love needs reminds us of the definition of love—an intense positive interest in an object, attention being at the heart of the experience. One authority trying to define esteem needs wrote: "Everyone needs to march at the head of someone's parade," an exercise that focuses the spotlight on the recipient. The experiences of self-actualization take an individual to the peak of attention experiences. Humans are "perpetually wanting individuals," and basic to all these needs is the need for *positive-focused attention*.

The Need for Positive-Focused Attention

The need for positive-focused attention has brought about the concept of *attention psychology*. Charles Derber[1] has made an analogy between the economics of a capitalistic society and the attention-getting process. The amount of attention available for any given individual is severely limited; Derber claims that it is a scarce commodity. He has advanced the idea that we are suffering with *attention starvation*. We will examine four cases of attention starvation.

Case 1: The Ungrateful Flower Seller

My Fair Lady is a musical of rare quality concerning the speaking of the English language. Professor Henry Higgins had made a wager with Colonel Pickering that he could take Eliza Doolittle, a Cockney flower girl, and change her patterns of speech so she could pass for a member of a royal European family. With Eliza boarding in the Higgins home, the professor taught, drilled, and worked with the girl, until he felt confident enough to put her to the test. He then escorted her to a glittering event at which she *was* accepted as royalty.

Returning from the function, Higgins and Pickering relaxed in the living room and engaged in an excited interchange of self-congratulation about the success of the evening. In the background stood Eliza, being completely ignored.

Pickering left the room, and Higgins, noticing Eliza, asked her to hand him his slippers, whereupon Eliza exploded. She had plenty to complain about, days of hard work, outbursts from the irascible Higgins, late nights, drills, and exercises—but that was not her complaint. She exclaimed in her exasperation, "I *will not be passed over.*"

Eliza was suffering from *attention starvation.*

Case 2: The Reputation of an English City

The city of Coventry, England, is known for its contemporary steel-and- glass cathedral constructed to replace the medieval building destroyed by enemy bombs in World War II. A second feature is the clock in the heart of the city, which at noon features a display of Lady Godiva making her celebrated ride to save her people from higher taxes. Included in the display is Peeping Tom, the only person who looked.

The third attraction of this city is its contribution to the English language in the statement, "Send him to Coventry." The statement came originally from the unpopular practice of billeting soldiers in private homes. The citizens of Coventry had such dislike for this procedure that they refused to have anything to do with the soldiers. Any person fraternizing with the soldiers would feel the wrath of fellow citizens.

Because of this attitude, if a soldier were stationed in Coventry, the attitude of the citizenry meant he was cut off from all social interaction. Consequently, men in the army dreaded an assignment to this city. So has come the dictionary definition of the saying: Send him to Coventry, i.e., to take no notice, isolate, or have no dealings with.

The saying gives another example of the penalties of the use of *attention starvation.*

Case 3: The West Point Way

An old adage says, "Silence is golden," but for James Pelosy it was horror. A cadet at the tradition-encrusted West Point Military Academy, Pelosy had been accused of cheating on an engineering exam. In the trial that followed before the West Point Honor Committee, despite Pelosi's insistence on his innocence and in the face of conflicting evidence, the committee convicted him of the charge. However, after reviewing the cadet's case, on the basis of the undue influence of the committee adviser, the superintendent of the academy overthrew the conviction that was made earlier.

But it didn't end there. The student body of West Point had a distinctive way of handling cadets they felt to be guilty of a breach of academy honor. For many decades it has been called "silencing."

Pelosy was compelled to live by himself in a room generally occupied by three. Each day he ate his meals in lonely silence at a table with places for ten, and in public he was ignored by his fellow cadets. During the nineteen-month period that followed, the ostracized student lost twenty-six pounds in weight. After his graduation, he remarked to a reporter, "I've taken a psychology course, and I know what isolation does to animals. No one at the Academy asks how it affects a person."

On graduation day the silence was broken as fellow cadets for the first time in nineteen months spoke to him and shook his hand. Commenting on the act of his fellow cadets in reaching out to him he said, "It was just as if I were a person again."

Though the academy psychologist might have limited his teaching to studying animals, the academy cadets have for a long time been aware of the power of *attention starvation*.

Case 4: Worse than Bread and Water

Of all the means devised by the minds of people for punishing their fellows, few will ever surpass the convict settlements established by England in Australia in the eighteenth century. One of the most notorious of these was the prison located at Port Arthur in Tasmania.

The guards frequently used the lash to flog the convicts. The floggings were an example of human inhumanity to other humans. The standard instrument was the cat-o'-nine tails which developed into a device called the knout described by an observer, "The knout was made of the hardest whip cord, of an unusual size. The cord was put into salt water until it was saturated; it was then put in the sun to dry; by this process it became like wire, the eighty one knots cutting the flesh as if a saw had been used."[2] This horrible instrument was used to inflict as many as 100 lashes on the backs of prisoners. Some of these floggings left the subject completely crippled.

Despite all these punishments, and the pain involved, they were not effective. At long last an effort was made in the notorious Port Arthur settlement to reform the punishment practices by building what was known as a "separate prison." The system had originally been suggested by the Quakers who hoped it would encourage the convicts to contemplate their souls and their misdeeds.

In this special building each convict was given his own separate cell. All was complete silence. The guards wore slippers so there would be no sound of feet on the floor. On the rare occasions when they were allowed to leave their cells each convict was compelled to wear a cloth cap with a cloth visor in which there were two holes for his eyes. When they went to church on Sunday, they sat in a box-like structure in which they could see the chaplain, but no one else. They had to live in complete silence.

The commandant of the prison at this time was Charles O'Hara Booth. Booth was convinced that flogging, ". . . often exasperates them and drives them to crime instead of reforming them." He preferred solitary confinement which he said, is "much dreaded . . . subdues them through boredom." He went on to claim that they came out of this solitary experience ". . . better than they went in."[3]

Booth had discovered that the worst punishment he could inflict on a convict, even worse than the dreaded semi-starvation diet of bread and water, was *attention starvation.*

One Effect of Attention Starvation on One's Personality

We have already noted the allusion by Derber to a capitalistic society, in which the law of supply and demand governs the amount of any commodity and the way that attention is not readily available: hence the concept of attention starvation. There seems to be ample evidence to show that, like the malnutrition which is suddenly discovered in an affluent society, attention malnutrition is widespread among us. It may even be a factor in the delicate line that divides sanity from insanity.

The governor of a state in Australia had arrived at the mental hospital to open a new wing. He was early and expressed the desire to wander unaccompanied around the extensive grounds. Clad in the elaborate uniform of an air marshal of the Royal Air Force, ceremonial sword at his side, he came upon a patient sitting on a garden bench. The governor took a seat alongside him and attempted to engage the man in conversation. The patient responded with an increasing irritation which he finally expressed:

Patient: "Who are you?"

Governor: "I am the governor of New South Wales."

Patient: "They'll soon knock that out of you. I thought I was Napoleon when I first came here."

The patient was a victim of paranoia, a mental disorder that takes two forms, a feeling that the subject is surrounded by people who are talking about him, or delusions of grandeur that he is the king of England, the president of the U.S., a famous actor, or some other noteworthy person.

One authority[4] has concluded that these psychotic reactions may come from "attention starvation" and the sufferer, in his/her mind, is creating the attention for which he or she longs by seeing surrounding people focusing their interest on him or her. In one's delusions of grandeur of being some world figure, a person is assuring himself or herself of the attention he or she needs. Derber points out that people need attention to maintain their sanity.[5]

How Attention Starvation Affects a Society

We are immediately faced with the reality that people not only need attention individually, but the ordinary functions of society are impossible without attention. As Derber puts it:

> Without attention being exchanged and distributed, there is no social life. A unique social resource, attention is created anew in each encounter and allocated in ways deeply affecting human interactions.

If this statement be true, our whole society may be endangered by attention starvation.

An example of the type of difficulty that comes to society through inattention is seen in the extraordinary series of events which took place in the U.S. some fifty years ago. On the last weekend in October 1938, Orson Wells presented a Halloween radio play. Referred to by one author as "a corny update of H. G. Wells's *War of the Worlds*," it told the story of a group of invaders from Mars who were alleged to have landed in New Jersey. The plan of the play was to present it as if the listener were tuned into a program presented by a live dance band. The broadcast was interrupted at intervals by news reports about "a huge flaming object, believed to be a meteorite," that had landed on a New Jersey farm. It further claimed that it was the first assault of an alleged full-scale invasion from Mars.

Panic seized sizable numbers of people. One report claimed that "at least a million of them were frightened or disturbed."[6] Fleeing from the "invaders," individuals fervently prayed, telephoned relatives, awakened sleeping children and headed out anywhere. One woman in hysterics tried to avoid a fate worse than death and endeavored to poison herself but was fortuitously saved when her husband found her and intervened. A number of miscarriages resulted from the broadcast. Suits amounting to $200,000 (1938 value) were filed against the producer, and an investigation by the Federal Communications Commission was threatened.

> attention (a-ten'sh n) n. Abbr. att., attn. 1. Concentration of the mental powers upon an object; a close or careful observing or listening. 2. The ability or power to concentrate mentally.

The whole "invasion from Mars" event was an illustration of the way many people pay attention, and fail to pay attention, to a complicated group of activities. Four times, once at the beginning of the program and three times throughout, disclaimers were made that the content was fictitious.

The Highest Hunger of All

The use of the metaphor of starvation calls attention to the biblical prophecy of Amos where the same figure of speech is used to describe the human need for spiritual attention. "The days are coming," declares the Sovereign Lord, "when I will send a famine through the land—not a famine of food or a thirst for water, but a famine of hearing the words of the Lord" (Amos 8:11, NIV). Here is spiritual attention starvation.

In Israel's experiences of famine while wandering in the wilderness, there was a lesson to learn, so in the Book of Deuteronomy, "He humbled you, causing you to hunger and then feeding you with manna, which neither you nor your fathers had known, to teach you that man does not live on bread alone but on every word that comes from the mouth of the Lord" (Deut. 8:3, NIV). In this recapitulation of their experience, God was telling His people that the famine, which was the plague of antiquity, could serve a godly purpose and remind them of the importance of spiritual values in the living of their lives.

Interesting, these are the same words Jesus quoted in His temptation, after He had fasted for forty days and when the tempter suggested that He should use His miraculous powers to assuage the hunger pains that had taken hold of Him by turning the loaflike stones of the Jordan desert into bread. Jesus took up the theme from Deuteronomy, "But he answered and said, It is written, Man shall not live by bread alone, but by every word that proceedeth out of the mouth of God" (Matt. 4:4). He was refusing to use His miraculous powers to provide food for physical hunger when the all-important spiritual hunger needed to have first consideration.

Later in His ministry, in the course of the Sermon on the Mount, Jesus enunciated the Beatitudes among them:

"Blessed are they which do hunger and thirst after right-eousness: for they shall be filled" (Matt. 5:6). These Beati-tudes have been referred to as the *heavenly octave*, and in this fifth Beatitude, Jesus used the craving of bodily hun-ger as a parable of the higher yearning after God with a spiritual hunger.

Abraham Lincoln once remarked to a friend, "I have been reading the Beatitudes, and can at least claim one of the blessings herein unfolded. It is the blessing pro-nounced upon those who *hunger and thirst after right-eousness.*" From his personal experience, the great man was able to acknowledge the spiritual hunger that he had experienced in his life.

It is to be expected that John's Gospel with its heavy emphasis on the mystical would take up the theme of spiritual hunger. We will later learn about the impor-tance of imagery in communicating truth, and in His ministry Jesus delivered a series of discourses in which He described Himself using such figures of speech as "I am . . . the Good Shepherd, Light of the World, the True Vine." Among these images was that of bread.

The occasion was a dialogue about the miracle of feed-ing the people. One of the issues raised was the feeding of their forefathers with the manna, and Jesus deftly turned the conversation concerning the "true bread from heaven," and went on to make His declaration, "And Jesus said unto them, I am the bread of life: he that com-eth to me shall never hunger; and he that believeth on me shall never thirst" (John 6:35). We will notice the way in which Jesus in terms of Maslow's theory of needs moves from the lowest level, the physiological hunger (bread), and moves to the highest self-actualization (never hunger).

There is a personal responsibility in all of this. The im-probable situation of the all-powerful and risen Christ seeking the attention of His creatures is presented in the apocalypse, "Behold, I stand at the door, and knock: if any man hear my voice, and open the door, I will come in to him, and will sup with him, and he with me" (Rev. 3:20). The result of the response to the Christ's pleading will be the experience of fellowship which is described in terms of eating a meal, ". . . sup with him, and he with me." In this experience the spiritual starvation has ended, satiated by the relationship with the risen Lord.

In Old Testament times there had been a promise of a day yet to be when there would be a solution to the problem of famine, "They shall not hunger nor thirst; neither shall the heat nor sun smite them: for he that hath mercy on them shall lead them, even by the springs of water shall he guide them" (Isa. 49:10). The last book of the Bible brings the finale to the whole problem of famine, "They shall hunger no more, neither thirst any more" (Rev. 7:16).

Attention starvation will set the theme for our consideration in this volume. It will remind us about needs of the human personality for attention from his or her fellow persons, and ultimately from God, who has promised in the words of the psalmist, "For he satisfieth the longing soul, and filleth the hungry soul with goodness" (Ps.107:9). We will later discover that this selfsame God has His own distinctive needs for attention from His creatures. The implications of these concepts will provide us with a fascinating topic for discussion in the following pages.

"Thou hast made us for Thyself and we are restless/ Till we find rest in Thee" (Augustine).

Notes

1. Charles Derber, *The Pursuit of Attention* (New York: Oxford University Press, 1983).

2. Robert Hughes, *The Fatal Shore* (London: Collins Harvill, 1987), 404.

3. Ibid., 403.

4. R. D. Laing, *The Divided Self* (London: Penguin, 1965).

5. Derber, 10.

6. Hadley Cantril, *The Invasion from Mars* (Princeton: Princeton University Press, 1947), 43-44.

2

Giving the Greatest Gift

"Love is an intense positive interest in an object."
—Dr. Smiley Blanton

"Men are rotten gift givers," so says Judy Hubbard who teaches a course on present giving. She explains that whether it is from lack of interest or acumen few men are practiced in the art of buying gifts, writing cards, or wrapping and presenting presents. Too often men choose chocolates, flowers, perfume, and lingerie which are not necessarily romantic presents. Since there may be a certain aura about silk pajamas, she says most wives would find breakfast in bed for a week the more romantic present. Judy says the latter shows love in action and that has more romance.

This woman is simply telling us something that most men know. I speak from personal experience. I am the world's worst. It seems that when the gift for giving gifts was given out I missed it. I am so bad that when I tell my wife I am going out to buy a present for her, a startled look comes over her face. She says, "Please keep the sales receipt so I can take it back," or "Please don't; I'd rather do it myself," or "Please don't bother—how much money would you like me to spend?"

What Do Women Really Want?

"What is the greatest gift a husband can give his wife?" I have asked hundred of wives this question and have been generally met with a puzzled silence. To help my subjects, I volunteer some information. "I can tell you what you don't want. You don't want diamonds, a lake house, a new home, or a round-the-world trip. It would be none of these things, even though you might think you want some of these baubles. The greatest gift a husband can give his wife is positive-focused attention."

In discussions with women in asking them about gifts from their husbands, one of the few responses is, "The thing I want most from my husband is love." As a Christian I am compelled to acknowledge the primacy of love. The essence of the problem is in asking what we mean by the word *love*.

I was delighted to learn in the course of a conversation with the famous psychologist O. Hobart Mowrer that he was interested in the nurture and culture of African violets. It so happened that at this particular time I had developed an interest in those temperamental little flowers and hoped my learned friend, so skillful in probing the human psyche, might know some secrets about these plants that had caused me so much concern.

It turned out that, as a fellow struggler in the horticultural enterprise, he had been through many of the same problems as I. As I shared my meager knowledge with my friend, I produced a newspaper clipping setting forth what were called "The Ten Commandments" for raising African violets. The last commandment was the clincher. It simply said, "Love them." I looked at my friend and asked: "Love an African violet? What next?"

The outstanding student of human nature smiled and gave me an answer that confirmed his insight as a student of human personality. "Don't you suppose that when it says to love an African violet, it means to look at them regularly, pay a lot of attention to them?"

All of this gives us a clue to the nature of love. A psychiatrist has said, "Love is an intense positive interest in an object," and as that loved object becomes aware of all the attention, a feeling of exhilaration follows. One dictionary definition of *attention* is "acts of courtesy or devotion, indicating affection, as in courtship." The word *love* itself can make an excellent acrostic:

Looking at the love object, focusing attention on the person. Turning one's eyes on the subject is the first and foundational aspect of attention giving.

Overlooking the weaknesses that don't appeal to you. After marriage, reality often begins to set in, and the not so obvious weaknesses emerge. These weaknesses should be *punished*! Punished with inattention as we overlook them.

Verbalize your affection. Tell the loved one how much you care for him or her. The spoken statement gives assurance to the subject that he or she is not being taken for granted. This open act is heightened in its effectiveness by the ratio of the number of people before whom the praise is given.

Energize your behavior. It has been said that love is something you do. Let your behavior give evidence of your love. *Demonstrate*—show by your actions.

Positive-focused attention is the key to the experiences of love.

The Foibles of Romantic Love

The word *love* can be used in many ways, and one of the most popular forms and strangely distorted forms is to be seen in what is called romantic love. The attention process is important because romance is a strange mixture of fantasy and reality, and attention is selective, focusing on one aspect of the total impression. This strange phenomenon is seen in the experience of the actor Orson Welles.

Welles had "fallen in love," he said, "madly ... in love." The object of his love was an Italian actress of whom he says, "She had a face like a spoon." He says, "I was blinded, unable to see ... she treated me like dirt. ... All she did was snarl at everyone. Everybody hated her. We detested each other." The relationship ran its ridiculous course until the actor was able to say, "I wasn't in love anymore, but I was stupefied by my own stupidity."[1]

This perversion of a wholesome love experience is an illustration of split attention. The actor was focusing his attention on one aspect of the experience. He wanted to "fall in love," and the negatives, looks, attitude, and relationships with other people were all ignored. Small wonder the affair was abruptly terminated when the actor discovered he was no longer "in love."

A similar illustration of love as split attention is seen in a pre-post marital perspective which may be stated as:

> *Before marriage:* The tacit contract of courtship is to overlook the loved one's faults and concentrate on his or her strengths.
>
> *After marriage:* The tendency is to reverse the process and minimize strengths, while criticizing weaknesses.

This splitting of attention is what can make a misery of a relationship that started with such high potential but has broken at some point.

Particularly Positive

Notice that it is a special type of attention. Some married people give their spouse *negative attention* which may be a different matter altogether. This is seen in the wife who frequently nags her husband. She is giving him attention, but it is certainly no reward. The husband who gets into a negative frame of mind complains about the way she keeps house, rears the children, prepares the meals, and wears her clothes. The boss who minutely examines his helper's work becomes what is known as a nitpicker. This attention is negative and may only serve to discourage the worker. In an effort to counteract this type of attitude, one of the statements of a successful motivator is, "Try to catch your assistant doing something right."

However, despite the rightful warning against negative attention, we should note that even negative attention may be sought by some people. One of my counselees was telling me of her problems with her marriage. She had filed for divorce but confided that she really didn't want to end the relationship. Well, why did she file for divorce? Her reply, "I wanted to get his attention." The problem was that her plan misfired, when her husband welcomed the proceedings.

The need for attention, any kind of attention, is shown in the experience of Carol Burnett when she was a sixth-grade girl:

> He was the most popular boy in the school and president of the sixth-grade class. I once got the feeling he kind of liked me, when I was walking home with Homay [Carol's girlfriend], and he came up behind me and snatched my sweater from my shoulders, threw it up a tree, shoved me a little, and ran off. As far as I was concerned, it meant only one thing. He loved me, too. Homay agreed wholeheartedly. I happily climbed the tree and retrieved my sweater from its branches.[2]

Some bad behavior of children is carried on at such an obvious level that it becomes clear that even in being punished the child may be gaining some gratifying negative attention.

Despite these negative exceptions the general rule remains that positive-focused attention is the crowning reward one individual can give another.

Varieties of Focused Attention

Any photographer can tell us how important it is for a picture to be focused. Properly focused pictures are sharp, but poorly focused pictures are fuzzy. Many fine cameras today have an automatic focusing action, but people who do not have automatic lenses know that focusing can be difficult. The latter has an equivalent in attention psychology. Investigators have concluded that there are three degrees of attention in which focusing is involved. These are:

Unfocused Attention

The type seen in settings such as shopping malls, a public gathering place, an airline terminal, and situations in which people are close to each other physically but aren't paying attention to each other.

Partly-Focused Attention

A situation in which some of the group are interacting with each other, while others physically present are paying attention to their own interests. This is illustrated by reference to the work of an industrious mother serving a meal for her family and their guests. She feels the important aspect of this experience is the quantity and distribution of the food. But she does not want to be left out of the conversation. While the group is involved in a spirited discussion, she is anxiously watching and refilling the plates, asking her guests about their reactions to the quality of the food.

She knows little of the content of the discussion. Occasionally, she pays attention and puts in her contribution to the conversation and may participate in the interchange, but she is mainly concerned with the food.

This may have a spiritual dimension to it. Huge numbers of devout Christians report the difficulties they experience with an errant thought during their experiences of prayer. Christopher Robin saying his prayers gives an excellent example of the difficulty with attention which starts as focused and all too easily drifts into a partly-focused mode.

> God Bless mummy. I know that's right.
> Wasn't it fun in the bath tonight?
> The cold's so cold and the hot's so hot.
> Oh! God bless Daddy—I quite forgot.
> If I open my fingers a little bit more,
> I can see Nanny's dressing gown on the door.
> It's a beautiful blue, but it hasn't a hood.
> Oh! God bless Nanny and make her good.
> Oh! Thank you, God, for a lovely day.
> And what was the other I had to say?
> I said "Bless Daddy," so what can it be?
> Oh! Now I remember it. God bless Me.

Martin Luther had his own problems in this area, and he considered problems of partly-focused attention; he made a down-to-earth suggestion about getting into the focused mode, "You can't stop the birds flying over your head, but you can stop them making their nests in your hair."

Focused Attention

That type of attention in which the attention-giver maintains a single focus of attention on one person. It is best demonstrated by the tete-a-tete in which one individual is talking to another and at least temporarily excluding any other person.

The unfocused, partly-focused, and focused situations are demonstrated in the biblical incident of Jesus visiting the home of Martha and Mary. Martha, the activist, was hard at work about the house while Mary took advantage of the situation and sat at Jesus' feet "listening to what he said." Martha complained to Jesus who gently rebuked her.

The three types of attention are to be seen in the incident:

(1) Unfocused attention.—Some of the people were curious villagers with little real interest who may have stood outside, occasionally peeking in the window and some in the room not paying attention, talking to each other in what we now call subgrouping.

(2) Partially-focused attention.—Martha was concerned about serving the meal, occasionally entering into the conversation. But Martha was distracted by all the preparations that had to be made. She came to Him and asked, "Lord, don't you care that my sister has left me to do the work by myself? Tell her to help me!"

Jesus voiced His gentle rebuke, "Martha, Martha, you are worried and upset about many things, but only one thing is needed."

(3) Focused attention.—Mary sat at Jesus' feet, and He commended her. "Mary has chosen what is better, and it will not be taken away from her"(Luke 10:38-42, NIV).

Are You a Wide-Angle or a Close-Up?

However, another element enters into taking a photograph, the focal length of the lens. Photographers use a number of different lenses among which are the wide-angle and the close-up. Even if it is properly focused, a wide-angle lens gives a broad view. These lenses are popular with tourists who wish to take a wide picture and include as much of the scene as they can and are particularly helpful when the photographer does not have room to back off.

People have different perspectives on life. Some take a wide sweep: they see little value in the close-up details of living. They are the wide-angled people.

A close-up lens on the other hand will focus in on one part of the broad picture. Movie cameras use a zoom lens that starts as wide angle taking an "established shot" and then zooms in close up to focus on one small portion of the total picture.

Most of us are wide anglers. We take a wide sweep in our view of life. If we are going to apply the laws of attention, we must learn the skills of close- up focusing.

The characteristics of the wide-angle personality and the close-up personality are:

Wide-Angle	*Close-up*
Sees people as a group.	Looks at what an individual sees.
Labels people in categories.	Realizes there are no two people alike.
Concentrates on what will influence a great number of people.	Asks what are the needs of the individuals.
Concerned about the environmental factors, influencing people.	Examines the internal motivations that need to be understood.
Adopts a hands-off attitude towards people.	Looks for ways to intervene and eradicate self-defeating behavior.
Uses the method of the public speaker, using suggestion to influence large numbers.	Uses the method of the counselor, focusing on one individual.
Uses broad generalities.	Focuses on small, particular element in personality

In a recent book about the Bingham family, a dynasty of Kentucky which was so wealthy and privileged and yet faced many internal family problems, the son spoke of his father, "My father loves humanity in general and no one in particular."[3] This is the stance of many wide-angle Christians who somewhat glibly state that they love the world but do little about focusing in on the individuals whom they encounter in daily life.

When we do "zoom in," we make some interesting discoveries. During World War II, German spies wanting to send information out of America used the microdot technique. To do this they photographed a page and then reduced it to the size of a period. This period was inserted in an innocuous letter at the end of a sentence. When the message reached its destination, it was enlarged to full size. Perceptive people see their fellows as microdots. The microdot could have been viewed as a flyspeck on the paper, but to the people who were prepared to take the close-up perspective, it was an invaluable message about human personality.

Positive-Focused Attention Is the Greatest Gift

While it is easy to give assent to this proposition concerning attention it is another matter to apply it to human behavior. If we accept the concept of wide- angle and close-up personalities, we will see the task is to help wide-angles change to close-ups. In the chapters that follow, we will consider the complexity of attention experiences.

The task of this book is to train people to use this knowledge of a fundamental need of human personality so they can discover their own potentialities. We may call these people *attention-getters*. To do this we will seek to change people from wide-angle to close-up, from unfocused and loosely focused to focused and always positive. We will embark on a program of developing the peculiar skills of the caregiver, a process we will undertake in successive chapters of the book.

CBS's renowned program "60 Minutes" ran and repeated a number of times the story of Gene Lang. Mr. Lang is a millionaire businessman. Invited to speak at a school in Harlem, he accepted and was worried sick about what he should say. As he stood to speak about the importance of staying in school, he suddenly heard himself announcing that each student who graduated would be given a grant that would pay their college tuition.

Mr. Lang interviewed the students who were interested and arranged to employ each person part-time, to keep an eye on each participant, and to call them regularly and check on them. The program has been enormously successful.

A number of students in the program were interviewed and asked about their reactions. Few of them mentioned the considerable sum of money that was involved, but some said directly, and others implied, the greatest gift they had received from Gene Lang was attention.

Like Gene Lang, we, too, can help to bring remarkable changes in human beings, when we learn the skill of applying *positive-focused attention.*

Notes

1. Barbara Leaming, *Orson Welles* (New York: Penguin, 1985), 440-42.
2. Burnett, 100.
3. Marie Brenner, *House of Dreams* (New York: Random House).
4. Leaming, 206.

3

Choosing Your Experience

"My experience is what I agree to attend to."
—*William James*

Communication is a matter of *who* says *what* to *whom, how*, with *what effect*, and is received with *what* attention. The communication skills used by humans can be conveniently divided into two broad categories. The first and most obvious being *expressive skills*. The aim of most communication programs is to make the student into a capable expressive communicator, and when we envision the finished product of such a program, we think of an orator, a brilliant writer, an actor, a singer, or an artist. But this emphasis does a disservice to the other type of communication skills which can be called *assimilative communication skills*. These are more frequently seen in the work of the student, literate individual, mathematician, and scientist, all of whose training has involved a wide use of assimilative attention in acquiring these skills.

Two Types of Attending Skills

Assimilative attention.—Takes place "inside the skin" (INS), the attention we feel compelled to pay or apply indirectly with

41

the hope of gaining information. These will be our focus in this chapter and chapters 4 and 7.

Expressive attention.—Is seen in activity "outside the skin" (OUTS), the attention we give in the hope of communicating with and influencing other people. The last chapters of the book will be given to this consideration.

The assimilative attention skills can in turn be divided into three types, *absorbing, active,* and *passive volitional* types of attention. We will consider each of these in turn.

Absorbing Attention

Absorbing attention is the type which is experienced in the process of reading an excellent book, listening to a spellbinding orator, or going into a hypnotic trance.

I have always had an interest in history and remember an occasion in my student years when I took the subway to the city to buy a textbook for a church history course. I purchased Lindsay's short history of the Reformation. Having completed the transaction I boarded the return train and began to read that fascinating book, almost missing the station where I had to exit.

In my room by eleven, I sat at my desk absorbed in my book. I missed my lunch, read on through the afternoon, missed my supper, and finally finished the book at nine in the evening. When I closed the covers of the volume, I was in a strange exhilarated state. I had been carried along by the fascinating writing and greatly enjoyed the passive assimilation experience.

My mother could never see any sense in music education, and without any internal motivations to push me towards this field of study, I grew into a musical illiterate. During my seminary training, it began to dawn on me that I would need to know something about church music, but I could never get excited about it. One Sunday afternoon I was returning from visiting one of the members of the church of which I was student pastor. I passed a Methodist Church outside of which a sign announced a performance of the *Messiah* on that Sunday afternoon. Never having heard the oratorio and deciding I had nothing better to do, I entered the church.

As I took my place the conductor stood before this chorus, he raised his baton, and they began to sing the "Hallelujah Chorus." I was overwhelmed. It seemed as if I were back at the beach engaged in the surfing I enjoyed so much, but surfing in music, the waves of sound came rolling over me, sweeping me along with it. The new, ever-mounting levels of voices upon voices made it an all-time peak experience for this music illiterate. I was again in the throes of absorbing attention that required no effort on my part.

Three Types of Assimilative Attention

Absorbing attention experiences.—These experiences call for no action by the attender who is carried along by the experience of attending without any conscious act of the will.

Active assimilative attention.—Experiences in which the subject concentrates on the process and is an active participant in the experience.

Passive volitional attention.—Experiences involving skills used indirectly by imaging or visualizing the desired change while in a relaxed state.

When I first tried to develop my writing skills, I decided the best way to do this would probably be to read the works of the great writers. So I commenced a process of reading every outstanding book I could lay my hands on. However, my readers will readily testify that I did not suddenly develop into a Sir Walter Scott, Charles Dickens, or Charles Read. In fact, I can't consciously recall a single skill I learned from my reading experience. Why? I became so interested in the reading process that my critical powers were laid on one side, and I lost interest in style, vocabulary, sentence structure, and other literary techniques. My absorbing attention experiences had defeated my efforts.

This is *absorbing attention*. It is the sort of attention that the speaker, singer, musician, and salesman longs to see in his or her listeners. The would-be communicator will have to learn the skills of making one's presentation so enthralling that auditors will be caught up in an absorbing attending experience. It is the experience of a member of your audience rushing up and exclaiming, "Why did you stop? I wanted you to keep on." This facet will be considered in a full treatment of expressive attention skills in later chapters of this book. In this chapter, we are focusing on what goes on within the individual in his experience of using his assimilative attention skills.

Active Assimilative Attention Skills

The importance of the second type of attending experiences, called active assimilative attention skills, is seen in the statement of William James who observed, "The faculty of voluntarily bringing back a wandering attention over and over again is the very root of judgment, character and will. An education which should improve this faculty would be the education par excellence."

With the present emphasis on expressive communication, it has become popular to look back with horror on the days when children were "seen and not heard," and educators have ushered in a new era of feverish, noisy activity. A silent student in a modern classroom obviously has a "personality problem." Everything is done to "draw him out" and to motivate him toward the goal of "self-expression." If he speaks up and contributes, even if he has nothing to say, all is well.

> The faculty of voluntarily bringing back a wandering attention over and over again is the very root of judgment, character

and will. An education which should improve this faculty would
be the education par excellence.—William James

After many years of teaching, I have reached the conclusion that much "self-expression" is mere undisci-
plined, unprofitable babble. On the other hand, some researchers have suggested that active assimilative
attention skills such as listening might be the activity
which furthers and expands the knowledge of a person
anxious to learn. Certain information can be acquired
only by careful listening. Comprehending the basic ideas
and concepts of subjects like music appreciation, speaking skills, and language demands that the learner have
well-formed attention skills.

Benefits from Active Assimilative Skills

Active assimilative skills are basic to the process of becoming a well-informed person. There are several areas
in human experience where these skills are of particular
importance:

- Widening intellectual horizons.
- Revealing hidden potentialities in personality.

We will consider each of these in turn:

Widening Intellectual Horizons

In the course of conducting conferences in which books
are sold, I have been amazed at two trends. The first is the
disproportionate number of women who buy books as
compared with men. It may be the nature of the books.
Personality development, psychology, marriage, and family life have a greater appeal for women. But many men,
who can, at the drop of a hat, quote baseball statistics,
football scores, or hunting and fishing seasons, are indifferent to our literary treasure house. "The world would
be better if leaders were selected not for their policies but
for what they read" (Joseph Brodsky).

The second thing that bothers me is the number of people who will comment, sometimes with apparent pride, "I never read a book." All the wonders of the world of books are lost to many people. It was recently reported that Emma Freud, the great granddaughter of Sigmund Freud, was the host of a British TV talk show with the title of "Pillow Talk." Clad in her pajamas, she sat with her guest on a double-size mattress. Asked about her famous great-grandfather she said, "I know nothing about the man—have never read a single book or article of his—so I don't know what he would say about the show."[1]

Emma Freud, the TV personality who has never read a word of a book or article by her illustrious great-grandfather, may be typical of much that goes on today. Many of the nonreaders will frequently add, "I just watch TV." If this is literally true I dread to think of the quality of their perspective on life. "A book can transform a life" (Alan Bloom).

It is a matter of attention. Reading demands concentration, but TV makes few demands on the viewer's assimilative attention skills. Television specializes in short snippets of information, frequently an oversimplification of a given situation. One TV viewer made the satirical comment, "It's a shame they spoil the commercials by occasionally small segments of news between them." Because of the proliferation of these obnoxious commercials the viewer learns *not to pay attention*.

> You may have tangible wealth untold
> Caskets of jewels and coffers of gold
> Richer than I you can never be—
> I had a mother who read to me.
> —Strickland Gillilan

So the person whose assimilative attention skills are mainly focused on television has two grave deficiencies in her life. She passes up the joy and thrill of reading great

books and develops the horrible habit of snippet attention. "All that mankind has done, or gained, or been: it is
lying as in magic preservation in the pages of books"
(Thomas Carlyle).

We need to remind ourselves about the spiritual gains
that can come to the believer. Paul said it well, "Till I
come, give attendance to reading" (1 Tim. 4:13). "Study to
show thyself approved unto God, a workman that nee-
deth not to be ashamed, rightly dividing the word of
truth" (2 Tim. 2:15).

The Other Assimilative Attending Skill

Of course, reading is not the only discipline that widens
our intellectual horizon. Another assimilative attending
skill, listening, is similarly important, but unfortunately
it is only casually employed in this function. If used properly, listening can open the windows of the mind, but if it
is to be effective, it calls for special attention skills.

It has been said that, "Listening is the lost L in learning." Written materials may be dull, boring, or uninter-
esting until we hear them. Reading a Shakespearean play
may not be easy, but listen to a gifted actor as he breathes
life into that cold print.

Simply by listening, we can access information that
would take years of research to gather. A lecturer may
have spent years investigating a given field of knowledge,
sifting the wheat from the chaff, gathering information
from different sources, and consolidating it into a cohe-
sive logical presentation.

There is a time lag in disseminating printed knowledge. By the time the author has gathered his information, written it down, had it appraised by a publisher, and
finally gotten it into book form, much of the information
in his newly published book is already dated. On the other
hand the lecturer has access to journals, studies, reports,

or even work in progress and can make this available to his listeners.

The interplay between a good speaker and his listeners plays an important role in conveying information. If a reader cannot understand the book he is reading, he may give up. By contrast the skillful speaker constantly senses and responds to her listener's reactions. If she becomes aware that her speaking level is obviously above or below their capacity to comprehend she can adapt her material to them. Moreover, there are possibilities of give and take questioning which make immediate clarification possible.

Active assimilative attention skills also develop an individual's creativity. The upsurge of interest in some of the old radio dramas has pointed out the part the listener plays in the radio presentation. We have come to believe that the visuals of TV are important in dramatic presentations. We must see it. *Not so!* Some radio enthusiasts speak about the "theater of the mind," in which the listener provides his own visuals. The secret of this is learning the skill of active assimilative attention.

One writer in the field of communication has made an appeal for people to spend more time listening. He pointed out that most people can remember only 25 percent of what they have read in just two weeks' time. What a tragedy if we have neither the capacity to recall what we have read nor listen carefully enough to retain what we hear. Both listening and reading are applications of active assimilative communication skills—an indispensable capacity for knowledgeable human beings.

Discovering Our Potentialities Through Active Assimilative Skills

Hypnosis is one of the most esoteric areas of psychology. Many claims are made for its use as a therapy, losing weight, handling pain, overcoming phobias, quitting smoking, developing self-motivation, recovering material from the unconscious, and a multitude of other uses. All of these are dependent on the capacity of the individual to pay attention to his hand, a light, or a similar object. The crucial aspect of inducing a hypnotic trance is for the subject to concentrate on a focal point. He is told that if his mind wanders he is to bring his attention back to the focal point. As one authority states it, "Hypnosis is a method of attention control."[2]

The Englishman James Braid popularized the use of hypnosis and gave the phenomenon its popular name which comes from the Greek word *hypnos*, which literally means sleep. After a wide experience, Braid felt the word was not appropriate and preferred the term *monoideism*. But the newer term never caught the public's imagination in the same way as hypnosis. There were also practical difficulties for the practitioner. It was far easier for the hypnotist to repeat, "You are gradually going to sleep, sleep, sleep," rather than the more cumbersome, "You are going into monoideism, monoideism, monoideism."

We do know that the person in a hypnotic trance is not asleep. In many ways the individual is more awake than she ever was previously. If she were to drop into sleep, the effectiveness of the procedure would be lost. Attention is a necessary ingredient in the process. There are psychological principles of suggestion and at the head of these stands "The Law of the Concentrated Attention."

If the theories of the hypnosis school be accepted, namely that it is possible to bring on a state of altered consciousness, and all of the outcomes are accepted, we must remind ourselves that it would not be possible to bring it to pass, if the individual did not have well developed active assimilative attention skills.

Passive Volitional Attention Skills

Practitioners of the art of hypnosis have often discovered an unlooked for outcome to the experience. After the subject has come out of the trance the practitioner might ask, "How do you feel?"

A frequent response would be, "I never felt so relaxed in my life before." The hypnotist would note this euphoric state. This statement contained within it a clue to the possibilities of attention in other areas of life.

In one conference of doctors it was stated that,

> It appears that stress could be implicated in about 20 to 25 percent of all patient visits in the United States each year. That's almost as frequent as the common cold. Then an important distinction was made, "There is a difference between stress and the common cold, however. The common cold is a disease. Stress is not a disease."

Whence came this nondisease that is so important in illness? One theory states that it is a carryover from our primitive forebears who lived in a hostile environment in which a saber-toothed tiger or a hostile native might at any moment appear to attack. In this moment of time the human could take one of two major courses of action. That person could choose flight or fight. But when confronted by a threat in modern society, neither of these courses are appropriate, and the situation brings about a stressed condition.

In a fascinating work, Dr. Herbert Benson has presented an alternative. He says, "When not used appropriately, which is most of the time, the flight or fight response repeatedly elicited may ultimately lead to the dire diseases of heart failure and stroke."[3] He moves on to consider another possibility, "If the flight or fight response resides within animals and humans is there an innate psychological reaction that is diametrically different?"

Benson answers his own question by pointing out there is a mechanism within humans that could save them from stress. He calls this the *relaxation response*. Of the four elements of this process (which we will discuss in the next chapter) two of them are, "(3) an object on which to dwell, (4) a passive attitude." These important steps constitute the essence of passive volitional attention.

An important part of this process is the use of imagery or visualization. One of the most successful biofeedback techniques is called hand warming. In this process the subject is able to learn how to raise the temperature in his hands and feet. The procedure involves the use of visualization as an oblique way of getting a message to the body to move blood to its different parts.

It has been shown that when people try to use force in focusing attention to make a hand warm they are not successful, because they are using active volition rather than passive volition. Two authorities heading up the Voluntary Controls Program in the research department at the Menninger Foundation explain the situation:

> One just tells the body what to do, usually by visualizing the desired state, then detaches from the situation—steps aside, gets out of the way so to speak—and allows the body to do it.
>
> Another example of the difference between active and passive volition is in falling asleep. If you try to force yourself to go to sleep you become more awake, and the harder you try the less you succeed, until finally you are exhausted and wide awake. With passive volition, however, you visualize and feel the body becoming quiet, the emotions becoming tranquil, and the thoughts stopping. Effort itself is turned off. Our normally involuntary and unconscious sections can often learn to behave in ways that are consciously chosen if we visualize what is wanted and ask the being (body, mind, brain, unconscious, or whatever) to do it.[4]

Study of the human brain shows that in its processes it becomes a mass of electrical activity, and this activity can be measured. These measurements have led to the formulation of different types of brainwaves, alpha waves, beta waves, theta waves, and delta waves. Three of these waves give indication of association with attention experiences. Beta waves are associated with external attention, alpha waves are characteristic in internal attention, and theta waves are partially involved with both internal and external attention. As a footnote to our considerations in this chapter, we should note that attention is not just something we do with our sensory organs, it goes much deeper and has to do with the function of our brains.

I once studied for a radio operator's license. Part of this involved learning the Morse Code, no easy task for me. When it came to examination time, it took several attempts before I passed. The task was to send and receive the code at the speed of thirteen words a minute. When I was examined, it was on receiving, and having passed, I queried the examiner as to when I would take the sending test. He replied that this was unnecessary. Anyone who could receive at thirteen words per minute would most certainly be able to send at that speed.

The lesson I learned was *it is much easier to send than it is to receive*. Assimilative attentional skills are not easy to learn and need instruction and practice, but they offer a great reward to the practitioner and will enrich one's life, expand one's intellectual horizon, improve one's powers of concentration, provide a person with a skill for handling stress, and give a person an overall improved quality of life.

Notes

1. "People," *Time*, April 4, 1988, 89.

2. Elmer and Alyce Green, *Beyond Biofeedback* (New York: Delta Publishing Co., Inc., 1977), 234.

3. Herbert Benson, *The Relaxation Response* (New York: Avon Books, 1975), 25.

4. Elmer and Alyce Green, 54.

4

Diagnosing
Attention Deficit Disorder

"You forget to pay attention to what is happening and that's the same as not being here and now."
—Aldous Huxley

What do AIDS, AD, ADD, and SAD have in common? Apart from the use of the letters *A* and *D*, very little it seems. AIDS (Aquired Immune Deficiency Syndrome), AD (Alzheimer's Disease), and SAD (Seasonal Affective Disorder) are altogether different from the psychological entity known as ADD (Attention Deficit Disorder which could be the greatest threat of all.

While many efforts are being undertaken to alert the American people to the threat of AIDS, AD, and SAD, nothing is being done to warn them about the threat that comes to the psychological aspects of life and affects the quality of the all-important interpersonal relationships which is commonly called ADD. However the well-kept secret has long been known to schoolteachers and suspected by parents.

Shakespeare, who had so many insights into human nature, was perceptive in diagnosing some of the problems of human personality:

> Lord Chief Justice to Falstaff, "You hear not what I say to you?"

Falstaff, "Very well, my lord, very well . . . it is the disease of not listening, the malady of not marking that I am troubled withal."[1]

This might be the most terrible of all diseases that can afflict the human personality, because it will affect both our internal equilibrium and relationships with other people. It needs our immediate attention because *attention demands our attention.*

Have We Been Calling It Maturity?

One perceptive researcher was interested in the commonly used term of *immaturity* to describe a personality problem seen in children and at other stages of life. The word *immaturity* literally means unripened and indicates some failure in personality development and has come to be loosely used in pop psychology. In a reconsideration of his previous work, Dr. Quay came to realize that in his review of the literature on child psychopathology that immaturity was, in fact, what has come to be referred to as Attention Deficit Disorder.

This use the term *immaturity* by Quay reminds us that one of the popular definitions of *maturity* is "the capacity to postpone pleasure." This definition makes it interesting to read a discussion of Attention Deficit Disorder and note the statement, "Research findings suggest that ADD children have strong inclination to seek immediate direct gratification."[2]

Recognition of the part played by attention in some of these problems has come slowly. It was not until the publication of the American Psychiatric Association's *Diagnostic and Statistical Manual III* (referred herein afterwards as DSM III) that the entity of Attention Deficit Disorder appeared and replaced that of Hyperkinetic Reaction. The emphasis had been on hyperactivity but now has come the emphasis on the attention aspects of the difficulty. An earlier researcher had pondered the fact that many of the behavior problems seen in children were really problems of sustained attention and really had to do with concentration and attention,[3] rather than the movement and activity generally called hyperactivity.

Attention Deficit Disorder

Confirmation of the veracity of Shakespeare's portrayal, and the new emphasis on attention, has come from the American Psychiatric Association's "Bible," DSMIII. One of the initial entries in this manual has to do with attention. It is *Attention Deficit Disorder*, a children's problem, and the preeminent indicator of the condition is the difficulty these children experience in paying attention. They give the impression that they are not listening or have not heard what they have been told.

The difficulty becomes most obvious in the classroom where the work of ADDS sufferers is often sloppy and performed in an impulsive manner. The disorder is frequently associated with hyperactivity but may be also seen without this component. In this simple form, there are two main manifestations of Attention Deficit Disorder:

Inattention.—At least three of the following takes place:
(1) often fails to finish things he or she starts,
(2) often doesn't seem to listen,
(3) easily distracted,
(4) has difficulty concentrating on schoolwork or other tasks requiring sustained attention, or
(5) has difficulty awaiting turn in games or group situations.
Impulsivity.—At least three of the following takes place:
(1) often acts before thinking,
(2) shifts excessively from one activity to another,
(3) has difficulty organizing work,
(4) needs a lot of supervision,
(5) frequently calls out in class, or
(6) has difficulty awaiting turn in games or group situations.[4]

In an effort to discover children who are suffering from Attention Deficit Disorder, a rating scale has been devised for parents to make an evaluation of their children. The story is told about a student who said that his family was so poor that none of them could afford to pay attention. Of course this is only a ploy, a play on words that ignores the possibility that it is not a matter of economics but of learning what some psychologists call "attending skills."

All of this information demonstrates the importance of an individual learning to pay attention, if he or she is going to develop his or her inner potential and acquire the knowledge that is so important in relating to other people.

Attentional Deficits

Trying to understand why certain children don't learn, some educators have pointed to this deficiency in paying attention. These children frequently seem to be looking at everything in general but taking notice of nothing in particular.

Some research suggested that the answer to this problem was to plan a schoolroom which would minimize distractions that capture the child's attention and cause the children not to pay attention. They enlarged the space between desks to remove distractions from other children, and built enclosed study cubicles where the children could be assigned in almost total seclusion. They used neutral colors on the classroom walls and removed factors that might distract attention. The teachers wore neutral colors and kept schedules to a predictable routine. The methods of teaching all aimed at having special stimulus value.

The effort was expensive, and it was hoped that this removal of distractions would raise the achievement level of the students. However, the gains were rather modest, and it becomes obvious that it is not the removal of distraction, but rather the heightening of the motivation of the student and development of attending skills that is important in dealing with this problem.

The Problem of Attention Deficit Disorder in Adulthood

All this discussion of children can all too easily lead interested parties to discuss ADD as a "childhood condition" and put it into the same category as mumps, chicken pox, or measles and see it as something to be endured in childhood days as part of the process of growing and to dismiss it with, "Oh, he will grow out of it." The onset of the condition may be early; one report speaks of "hyperactive toddlers" with the peak age at which children are referred for professional help coming at about ten or eleven.

One of the reasons for this emphasis on the childhood aspects of ADD is that it was observed by the schoolteachers who became pivotal figures here. One researcher notes,

> The symptoms of ADD are variable and may not be noted during the clinical interview, so diagnosis often depends upon reports by parents and teachers. Teachers' reports are considered particularly valuable, because of teachers' greater familiarity with the age-appropriate behaviors and because they often observe children's responses to tasks that require sustained attention, persistence, and organization.[5]

In adulthood this school-room screening process no longer exists, and the individual lacking in attention skills may go on his merry way missing some of the most important experiences of life and becoming the despair of those who wish to communicate with him.

Although Attention Deficiency Disorder is primarily

seen in childhood, where the symptoms stand out by comparison with the other children in a school-room situation, the *Diagnostic and Statistical Manual of Mental Disorders* notes that the problem may persist into adolescence or adult life. This facet has been ignored in the past, and in the future, there will probably be much said about Attention Deficit Disorder in adulthood. Taking the criteria of adult manifestations of Adult Attention Deficit Disorder, it is possible to formulate a rating scale such as that which follows that will help us to personally evaluate our own or other people's condition. To take the test, mark each item with (1) never, (2) sometimes, and (3) frequently.

Adult Rating Scale

Check the number that describes you.
(1=never, 2=sometimes, 3=frequently)

Finds it difficult to concentrate.—Poor reading, poor participation in conversation, doesn't listen well to lectures and reports.

Restless and fidgety.—Taps fingers, swings legs, shifts chair.

Quick tempered.—Argues, fights, sometimes violent, loses control

Poor impulse control.—Low frustration tolerance, cannot delay gratification, acts on the spur of the moment.

Mood changes.—Changeable moods, usually brief ups and downs.

Poor organization inability to complete tasks.—Doesn't plan well, jumps from one task to another.

Low stress tolerance and overactivity.—Have "emotional thin skin," make "mountains out of molehills."

If in the answering of these items you made a score of fifteen or more, you might need to give some consideration to first item, "Finds it difficult to concentrate," which may be the key indicator of the difficulty and gives us a clue as to where we might need to start in handling ADD in adults. The rest of the items may be an answer to the people who complain about "focused attention."

The manifestations that go along with the lack of attention are those that can upset our relationships with others. If I maintain, "The skill of living is the skill of relationships," there may be horrendous possibilities. The first and major item in the test will be the focal point of our discussion.

As part of a battery of listening tests, participants were examined to find out what proportion of lecture material they had retained. The results revealed that, on tests given immediately after the listening experience, these professional people could recall only about 50 percent of what they had heard. What might have been the results had the tests been given a month or even a week later?

If a patient reported to his doctor that he was retaining only half the food that he ate, the alarmed physician would take steps to immediately remedy the situation. Yet if this same person were to admit that he was unable to recall more than half the information passed on to him, nobody would be very concerned.

If a college student were so physically ill that she could only attend half of her classes, she would probably seek permission to drop the course and ask for a refund of fees. However, indifferent attending skills could cause the same results—failure to retain fully half the material presented by the teacher. In terms of economics, her impaired attending skills might conservatively be estimated to cost her a thousand dollars or more a year, as well a sizable segment of life that was lost and could never be recaptured. It becomes clear that while we have given consideration to Attention Deficit Disorder in childhood, we have apparently ignored the problem in adults.

Any marriage counselor will tell of the high number of

husbands and wives who complain, "My husband doesn't listen to me," or "My wife just talks and talks and talks. I can't get in a word edgeways." Children constantly complain their parents don't listen to them, and parents face the same type of difficulties.

A group of women sat around the darkened room in a state of expectancy. They had gathered for a seance, and the medium addressed them, "Is there any loved one who has passed on with whom you would like to make contact?"

Mrs. Meeves quickly responded, "Never mind about those in the hereafter. Can you help me communicate with my teenage son?" It is merely a joke, but it does make a point.

It is frequently said that communication is the lifeline of family life. The available research seems to indicate that we may need to focus more on the attentive aspects of communication. There is apparently a strange contamination which comes into the family from members who give indication of behavior generally seen in ADD. One study showed that in this type of family there was greater difficulty with alcoholism and sociopathy in the fathers and mothers of these families.

What can we do about Attention Deficit Disorder? In the chapter that follows we will consider some of the activities which can be undertaken in an effort to cope with Attention Deficit Disorder.

Notes

1. Second part, *King Henry IV*, act I, scene 2, lines 136-40.
2. Ibid. 50.
3. Ibid., 34.
4. *Diagnostic and Statistical Manual of Mental Disorders* (Washington: The American Psychiatric Association, 1980), 43-44.
5. Ibid., 69.

5

Learning Assimilative Attention Skills

"That basic muscle attention which is after all, the psychological equivalent to cardiac fitness."
—Coleman

World War II brought with it a new word for most of the world—*blitzkrieg*. One man said that some believed the architect of this warfare concept was Heinz Guderian who wrote a book urging the use of independent armored formations with strong air and motorized infantry support. These formations quickly penetrated enemy lines and encircled vast bodies of men and weapons. Adolf Hitler accepted Guderian's theories and the rapid incursions into Poland, the Lowlands, France, and the Soviet Union in the early days of the conflict were in a large measure due to the theories which Guderian set forth in his book *Achtung! Panzer!* or in English *Attention! Tanks!*

Although England's Winston Churchill was a pioneer in the use of the tank in World War I and France's Charles de Gaulle an expert in tank tactics, they were left behind in the development of this new and special way of using armor. If only they had paid attention to Guderian's book with its appropriate title *Attention! Tanks*, the dictator Hitler might have been stopped in his tracks, and the world spared the horrors of World War II.

This failure to pay attention might be symptomatic of the general malaise that has fallen over the population and has only recently been recognized by the American Psychiatric Association, whose members were faced in the first place by schoolteachers who were being driven to distraction by inattentive students. The parents to whom the teachers reported the problem shrugged their shoulders and muttered comments to the teachers like, "I thought all children behaved like that," or "You think he's inattentive, you should see my husband in the house." This latter statement reminded us that the Attention Deficit Disorder is an unrecognized plague of epidemic proportions.

It has been estimated that 3-10 percent of all American children have ADD. In its two forms with or without hyperactivity, it is more frequently seen in conjunction with hyperactivity than the other way around. Strangely, too, it seems to be sex related and is more frequently seen in boys than it is in girls, with eight to ten boys for each girl with the disorder.

Confronted with the problems of Attention Deficit Disorder in children, the natural, common attitude is to take the child to a medical doctor. The expectation of the parent or teacher is that the doctor will write a prescription for medicine that will do the trick. Most doctors are ready to do this with such drugs as Dexedrine, Ritalin, Cylert, or Tofranil being the most frequently used. As with all chemicals there is the problem of side effects. There are parents who are suing schools for the damage that may have been done by some of these drugs. One somewhat skeptical psychologist has stated this medical philosophy as, "Sit still and take a pill."

By defective attention within the individual and those around them were they hurt—and by the abundant attention given and received will they be healed. One psychologist has noted there is no physical difference in the brain chemistry between the people who have the capacity of high-powered attention and those whose minds go wandering off at any opportunity. His approach is to see attention as a mental muscle and develop it accordingly. This is the plan that we will follow. As we have previously noted, most of the diagnostic work in this field has been done with children. Similarly the task of doing therapy has focused on ADD children. In our effort to alert people to the prevalence of attention deficiencies in the adults, of our society we will turn to some of the nonchemical methods that have been successfully used with children and see if some of these can be adapted to adults. What follows is an attempt to do this.

Learn a Relaxation Technique

In one study a group of eighteen children, both boys and girls, were selected because of their inability to adjust to the regular school programs.[1] They were divided into two groups, one of which became the control group and the other the subjects for the project. These subjects were given relaxation training following the program suggested in Benson's relaxation response technique.[2] The result was a significant decrease of 60 percent in the nonattending behaviors in the children who learned Benson's relaxation response technique.

Anyone can learn a relaxation technique. It will help you to obtain a copy of my book *The Awesome Power of the Healing Thought*.[3] In the appendix of the book there is a script which can help you make a cassette tape you can use to enter upon a relaxation experience. The three requirements for a good experience are: (1) *A quiet environment.*—The best location will be a spot where you will not be likely to be disturbed. (2) *A comfortable position.*—Although you need a comfortable position you should not lie down, because you will have a tendency to go to sleep. This is not your aim. Sleep is a different state from relaxation and undesirable. Just make sure you are in a place where you feel comfortable. (3) *An object to dwell on.*—As you progress through this experience you'll be led by the voice on the cassette through a series of stages. Ultimately you'll be guided to focus on a statement from the Bible. Following this leading is part of the training to improve your assimilative attention skills.

The reporters of the study with the children say, "Past studies were reviewed in which relaxation training helped children to improve levels of attention, classroom behavior, and other cognitive and academic performances."[4] An incidental benefit that may accrue from the relaxing experience for an adult may be a reduction in blood pressure, a problem which has proved responsive to this technique. "That basic muscle attention which is after all, the psychological equivalent to cardiac fitness" (Goleman).

Engage in Self-Monitoring

Research with children diagnosed as Attention Deficit Disorder indicated one method of therapy was to give them certain tasks to perform and required that they record how much of the time they were "on task" by paying attention. The researchers discovered the children's behavior improved so that the number of tasks they completed were doubled.

These self-monitoring procedures would offer some interesting possibilities in working with adults. As a boy, I belonged to the Boy Scouts. We played a game called Kim's Game which came from the story of the training of Rudyard Kipling's famous Indian boy. The game is still used by the Boy Scouts in teaching communication skills.

The instructor pulls back a cover over the table and reveals a number of items which are shown to the participants for a period of time, say two minutes. The cover is then replaced and the participant writes down the items he can remember. The exercise is repeated with different items and reduced viewing periods.

You can get some friends together and play Kim's Game. In this experience there would be the number of items to be viewed for an established period of time, and then checked on the number remembered. This procedure could possibly parallel the results of the experiment with the children and help to strengthen your assimilative attention skills.

Use Exercise as a Factor in Building Attention Skills

At least one bona fide study of treating Attention Deficit Disorder in children has discovered that programs of exercise have helped to overcome the problem. The study was called "Running Can Modify Classroom Behavior." One observer noted, "She (K. C. Bass) considers running to be viable as a treatment for children's attention span and impulse control problems."[5]

This same exercise factor can probably be effective in adult subjects. Studies have already shown the physical and psychological values of aerobic exercise. However, to be effective in building attention skills, it needs to be planned and participated in regularly with clear objectives. Consider the plan of Henry Adams.

Henry Adams's Exercise Program

Objective.—To undertake a program of exercise that will increase my cardiovascular fitness and general health, but an overarching effort will be to develop my attending skills. This will involve careful planning and concentration on the details of the activities.

Plan of Action.—(1) For the first two weeks I will walk three miles on Monday, Wednesday, and Friday in thirty-six minutes in the first week and increasing speed to thirty-four minutes the second week.

(2) In weeks three and four, I will walk two miles four days a week in thirty-two minutes in week three and increasing speed to thirty minutes in week four.

(3) In weeks five and six, I will walk two and a half miles four days a week in thirty-nine minutes in week five, and two and a half miles a week for five days in thirty-eight minutes in week six.

(4) Following week six, I will enter upon a regular program as set out in Cooper's book *The Aerobics Program for Total Well Being*.

Following this program, we will discover the interrelatedness of body and mind and the way exercising one's body can at the same time help to build the assimilative skills. Of course, as important as the physical exercise itself will be, the planning of the program and the follow-through will exercise the intellectual muscles. Many years ago, Paavo Nurmi, a Finnish winner of the Olympic marathon on a hot Paris day, is credited with acknowledging, "What I am, I am because of my mind." Attention is the key ingredient.

Keep Your Eye on the Ball

Australian aborigines are a unique people. In their primitive state they wear no clothes, cultivate no crops, and build no houses. Living their nomadic existence, they periodically move out. This nomadic practice is referred as going "Walk about." Yvonne Goolagong, the outstanding tennis player, is a charming person who not only played a remarkable game of tennis that put her at the top of women's tennis but charmed people with her gracious manner.

Yvonne is part aboriginal and has sometimes demonstrated this by the way she expresses herself. After being defeated in an important match, she was interviewed and asked what had happened to her. Her face lit up with her charming smile and said, "I went walk about." She was saying that she had fallen heir to a frame of mind that ruins players of ball games. The constant exhortation is, "Keep your eye on the ball." They have to realize the power of focused attention.

If you play a ball game you will have a wonderful opportunity to practice your attention skills. The outcome will be improved skills in your favorite sport, but you will also develop the attention skills that can make you much more effective in your relationship skills.

Stretch Your Mental Capacities

One effective technique teachers have used in teaching attention skills is to present material to be learned and to make it particularly interesting. Vocabulary building opens opportunities. Word-meaning studies will provide a basic tool for the student. They are equality effective for adults, many of whom develop a deep interest in studying words. An excellent source is *Reader's Digest*, which carries a monthly item called "It Pays to Enrich Your Word Power." What follows is a page similar to the following:

Building Your Vocabulary

Your vocabulary is very important and the more precise the definition of a word the more effectively you use it. Select the meaning you think is correct.

GRIT—A: biscuit. B: temper. C: spite. D: pluck.
FAZE—A: to eliminate. B: disturb. C: blur. D. endanger.
TOXIC—A: bitter. B: foul smelling. C: remedial. D: poisonous.
PANACEA—A: uproar. B: praise. C: cure-all. D: overall view.
CALLOW—A: tough. B: lacking depth. C: inexperienced. D: sickly yellow.
ABRIDGE—A: to condense. B: arch or bend. C: join. D: cross.

ENIGMA—A: nonsense. B: complication. C: puzzle. D: blemish.
INORDINATELY—A: rarely. B: unexpectedly. C: excessively. D: unsuitably.
FRACTIOUS—A: unruly. B: splintered. C: crooked. D: frail.
PRESUMPTUOUS—A: hopeful. B: insolent. C: probable. D: decisive.

Answers

GRIT—D: Pluck; unflinching courage or determination, as "The man demonstrated real grit in the way he withstood his illness."

FAZE—B: To disturb; upset. Generally used in a negative sense; as "not to be fazed by a problem." Old English fesen (put to flight).

TOXIC— D: Poisonous, destructive. Greek *toxikon* (poison).

PANACEA—C: Cure-all, remedy for all ills and difficulties.

CALLOW—C: Inexperienced, unsophisticated, immature.

ABRIDGE—A: To condense, shorten by omitting words without changing the meaning.

ENIGMA—C: Puzzle; riddle; baffling problem, inscrutable or mysterious person.

INORDINATELY—C: Excessively, immoderately.

FRACTIOUS—A: Unruly, hard to manage.

PRESUMPTUOUS—A: Arrogant, unduly confident.

Assignment

Now take a piece of paper and write ten sentences using each of these ten words.

Exercises with vocabulary building can be particularly profitable. Purchasing a "word calendar" which encourages the learning of a new word each day would be a good investment. Note, too, that writing it down is an important part of the process. John Adams said, "A pen is certainly an excellent instrument to fix a man's attention and improve his ambition."[6]

Of Winston Churchill, President John Kennedy once commented that in World War II, he mobilized the English language. This master of English, speaking of his writing, told of the part that attention played as he commenced a book on history.

Churchill penned a letter to his beloved Clementine in which he stated, "I cannot help getting very interested in the book. It is a great chance to put my whole case in an agreeable form to an *attentive audience*."[7]

As he reacted to this anticipated attention, he immersed himself in his work and his own personal experience of focusing his attention did something for him. He wrote another letter to his wife, "The more I do, the more I feel the need of doing." This caused him to widen the scope of his project. From his commencement of his work in 1928 until its conclusion in 1931, he industriously labored, until he completed his epic six-volume *The World Crises*.

In this study of attention in action, we notice the way attention motivated Churchill; then by using his own powers of attention, he motivated himself to extend his creativity to the profit of many people. The power of attention had come the complete circle.

Exercising the Attention Muscle

The use of the analogy of attention being a mental muscle brings to mind the experience of a man long associated with athletics. His name is Tom Landry, and in his position as coach of the Dallas Cowboys football team, he was highly successful.

Landry was sometimes referred to as the Great Stone Face. One commentator noted that Landry's expression vacillated from "Where am I?" to "Did something happen?" Called a "cerebral coach," he was often chided because, while the fans were roaring their heads off, he was standing on the sidelines looking at his clipboard, giving the impression that he had no interest in the play that was driving fans and players wild.

Explaining his attitude Landry stated,

> I think you have to train yourself to concentrate, and that is what I am doing on the sideline during the game. I don't see the game the way the fans do. I'm one play ahead all the time. While the team is running one play, I'm looking ahead, planning the next one. I suppose that's why I don't react to a play the way the fans do.[8]

Landry is an excellent example of instrumental attention. He could be described in the words of one psychologist speaking of attention skills, "able to put constraints on what they do. In other words, they can buckle down to the job at hand, no matter how many more appealing distractions tempt them."[9] This should be your aim in developing your assimilative attention skills.

No sooner has a therapy program with ADD children been contemplated than the question arises as whether medication or behavioral methods are the best. The argument is that medication is so much simpler. One study by Trualicka has suggested that medication might even bring more rapid immediate results, but in the long run, "The effectiveness of the two approaches seemed to be roughly equivalent."[10] Such a conclusion should be a great encouragement to someone who seeks to help his fellow human being to develop his attentional skills by the use of behavioral methods.

Notes

1. Charles Schaefer, Howard Millman, Steven Sichel, and Jane Willing, *Advanced Therapies for Children* (San Francisco: Jossey Bass, 1986), 351.

2. Herbert Benson, *The Relaxation Response* (New York: William Morrow, 1975).

3. John W. Drakeford, *The Awesome Power of the Healing Thought* (Nashville: Broadman Press, 1981), 161.

4. Schaefer, Millman, Sichel & Willing, 351.

5. C. K. Bass, "Running Can Modify Classroom Behavior," *Journal of Learning Disabilities*, 1984, 360-64.

6. *John Adams's Diary*, November 14, 1788.

7. Martin Gilbert, *Churchill* (New York: Doubleday & Co., 1980), 81.

8. Larry Wood, "Landry: Supreme Commander," *American Way*, September 1983, 76.

9. David Goleman, "Concentration," *Vogue*, September 1985, 345.

10. Schaefer, Millman, Sichel, Willing, 377.

6

Giving Family Attention

*"Those people who are able to afford it keep
a flapper in their family."*
—Jonathan Swift

Sitting upright in the uncomfortable chair, Mrs. Dill is obviously ill at ease in the principal's office. Mr. Renton, seated across the desk, has been through this experience many times before, but he never finds it easy. Tom, Mrs. Dill's fifteen-year-old, was caught handing over a packet of crack to another student; hence the interview.

Greeting formalities completed, Mrs. Dill answers an unasked question, "Mr. Dill couldn't come. He had business out of town."

"Did you and your husband talk about this matter before he left?" asked Mr. Renton.

"No we didn't, . . ." Mrs. Dill trails off as the tears begin to roll down her cheeks, "I never seem to be able to catch his attention."

Mrs. Dill has highlighted the heart of numerous difficulties in families: the lack of giving and receiving of attention.

An organization may be defined as the coordinated activity of an interdependent group of people within which communication occurs as attention is given and received.

Nowhere is this more clearly seen than in the organization which we call the family.

Studies in organizational life have shown that communication takes place on at least three directions—lateral, downward, and upward. Within the family the lateral communication will more frequently be between husband and wife, while the upward and downward communications will generally happen between the parents and the children.

Lateral Communication

Lateral communication describes the interchange of messages between two people at similar executive levels of an organization. Though they belong to the same institution, they may build their own empires and in the process fail to give attention to each other. In this way they ignore both the communication and interdependency aspects of organizational life.

A similar situation exists in the family unit, but there are some distinctions which make lateral communication more critical in the family than it is in any other forms of organizational life. Husband and wife are ideally a partnership, "Remember that you and your wife are partners" (1 Pet. 3:7, author's paraphrase), and this partnership is particularly important, because in marriage persons have become "one flesh," a rich expression implying a deep communication. This relationship lays the foundation for all the later communications in the family, and the basis they build will, in a large measure, determine the whole structure of communication that will characterize that particular family unit. "When a girl marries she exchanges the attentions of many men for the inattention of one" (Helen Rowland).

Consider executives of the business world in their lateral relationships following marriage, when the children

come along, the executive and his wife may gradually begin to move in two different directions. The wife may
commence on the pathway of becoming a supermother,
building a domestic empire with little place for her husband. Meanwhile, her husband is trying to carve out a
place for himself in the business world. As he applies himself to his task, it may seem to the family members that
he only comes home at a late hour to eat and sleep before
venturing forth the next morning into the world of business. These two different focal points can play havoc with
the lateral communications within the family.

Conversation is communication at its most elemental
level, but unfortunately husband-wife conversation is a
lost art! So say many observers of the passing scene as
they contrast the spirited tete-a-tete of yesteryear with
the pathetic conversational efforts of people at a contemporary gathering.

If you want to see how badly the conversational art has
deteriorated, merely look in on a husband and wife. Go to
a restaurant and look around the tables where a man and
a woman are looking into each other's eyes and excitedly
carrying on a spirited conversation—they're probably not
married.

On the other hand, if they give the appearance of being
a couple of strangers who have wandered in at about the
same time and the maitre d' has placed them at the same
table, and they are eating with a quiet earnestness and
silently working their way through the meal, there's a
good chance they're husband and wife. Bound by a sol-
emn marriage vow to be permanently joined together
they are conversationally separated from each other by a
yawning chasm. For example, Henry VIII and his wife
Anne Boleyn: ". . . by his *wounding inattention* to his wife
Henry made his dissatisfaction clear" (Ericson).

Strangest of all, when these two do communicate, some

strange things happen, and it is not the ever-present mother who dominates the communication process. One researcher tells of his findings from investigating modern families,

> In my field studies of one hundred and fifty families, I found that fathers were interrupted less often when they spoke and were listened to with greater respect and patience. They also exercised greater control over the topics that were discussed and were more successful in gaining the focus of attention when they sought to do so.[1]

When we divide husbands and wives into the roles of *attention-giving* and *attention-receiving*, it has apparently continued to be the expectation of the father that he will be the *attention-receiver* and the mother that she will be the *attention-giver*. If the marriage is to achieve its potential, husband and wife will have to learn to accept equal responsibility and the development of an equitable distribution of the roles of attention-receiver and attention-giver.

The conversational art requires thought, work, and above all, the application of attending skills by both participants, but it's an art that once mastered will enrich a husband-wife relationship. If you feel the interaction between you and your spouse is slowing down, why not try some interactional attention stimulators? Some examples follow:

• Let your spouse save face. People sometimes make foolish statements which are obviously incorrect; you don't have to put your partner right—*keep listening*.

• Be as pleasant and friendly with your husband or wife as you would with a stranger, and don't forget to *listen*.

• *The honest "I don't know"* is often the best reply to some question about a matter in which your information is limited—then *listen*.

• People are always more interested in themselves than they are in you—so *listen.*

• As your spouse talks, formulate a question that will encourage him or her and then *listen for the answer.*

• Play conversational tennis, seeing how adept you can become in hitting the conversational ball back to your mate and wait for a return *by listening.*

• Watch for warning signals, be sensitive to your partner's reactions. If you are not doing so well, *try listening for a while.*

The mention of conversational tennis reminds us that the game of tennis provides an excellent analogy for both the communication problem and its solution. The problem is seen in a game between two aggressive male players who give the impression that they might be two knights of old who are engaged in a duel to the death. The serve is like a cannonball being fired, followed by the vicious return and the devastating smash. The two would-be conversationalists in this instance are out to win no matter what and in the process anxious to cut each other down.

The solution to the problem is seen in the game of social tennis played by two genteel women. Cannon-ball serve, vicious return, and killing smash are all bypassed as these two work at each gently, directing the ball to the other player and taking great delight in the length of time they can keep the rally going. This type of conversation is a joy and a delight that leaves the participants with a satisfied feeling of well-being.

Upward and Downward Communication

Downward communication in organizational life is the message the executive wishes to pass along to the rank and file members of the organization. With the aid of public address systems, bulletins, conferences, and memos, the executive tries to distribute information concerning the enterprise in which they are involved. Some studies have revealed a great loss in downward communication in the process of which as much as 80 percent of the information may never reach its destination.

Within the family the downward communication processes have their own distinctive problems as parents try to communicate with the children. The age of the children is an important factor here. One father listening to the constant prattle of his four-year old commented, "Talk! Talk! Talk! Thank heavens, in a few years he'll be a teenager, and he won't say two words."

But when those adolescent years come, a parent faced with incommunicado teenagers may have some troubled moments. A father sitting at home and watching the technological miracle of pictures and sound beamed millions of miles from the moon to the earth, mentally contrasts this communication feat with his difficulty of getting a message across the living room to his son Jimmy.

Upward communication takes place as members of the organization try to get their messages up to the higher echelons. This is the most difficult of all communication and it takes a lot of work on the part of the leader to discover what the rank and file are thinking. It has been said that a top-line executive needs to spend 40 percent of his time getting feedback from his organization.

Attention has been called the "interactional currency," and this currency can be utilized for developing communication experiences as is demonstrated in negotiating with an obstreperous adolescent. The negotiation technique has long been used in situations where differences exist—international diplomacy, labor management disputes, ethnic or religious controversies. Now of recent days the method has been introduced into family situations. The great advantage of the negotiation method is the application of the "interactional currency"—attention to the situation. The following are a group of principles that can be used in communicating with adolescents.

The setting is an important factor in giving attention.— Let the session take place in a room where there are no distractions, no TV, no telephone. Remember his limited attention span has probably brought on the difficulty. Remove the possibility of intrusions.

Remember it is positive attention.—Much of your subject's arguments will sound unreasonable, if not downright impertinent, but make allowances for the brashness of immature youth. If he loses his temper, he is going to be shamed by your self-control.

Focus attention on your own failures.—That will grab his attention in a hurry. If we acknowledge mistakes, it will prepare the way for dialogue.

One father who had previously been particularly rough on his son said, "Jim I was wrong. I shouldn't have lost my temper. I'm sorry."

To his amazement the boy responded, "I shouldn't have taken the car without asking."

Turn attention to the non-negotiable matters.—We can't negotiate whether or not to obey the law. The teenager must learn to respect the legal boundaries. This painful but necessary boundary must be set up.

Demonstrate attention by the way you listen.—Remind yourself of the power of attention. He's often convinced that he has been on the receiving end for a long time. You should make him feel his time has really come. Fight back every impulse to interrupt. Listen, listen, listen. Just give a short response of "Oh," "I see," or "You sure have a point there."

Let all-powerful attention do its work. You may be surprised at the way in which he will talk himself out of some of the ideas he previously held.

Call attention to his or her ability to reason.—When he or she asks, "Why?" it isn't enough to reply, "Because I say so." Don't call attention to weak arguments or make sarcastic remarks. Use good-natured questions that will help her face her own inconsistencies. Ask her about her recommendations.

Direct attention to a new train of thought.—"Have you thought of this?" "What will you do if this arises?" Sometimes an anecdote will help, "I once knew a fellow . . ." Reference to a newspaper cartoon or story may help to show that the problem you two are facing is part of the universal human condition.

Pay attention to the act, not the person.—When "Junior" does something foolish, don't say, "You're stupid; that's not the way to go about things."

The better way would be, "I love and respect you, but I think that action was wrong. Nevertheless, I love you, even if I don't like what you are doing."

Learn to negotiate with your adolescents. It will call for patience and understanding, but your judicious use of attention will pay off in the long run.

Maybe We Need Flappers

In the course of his peregrinations, Lemuel Gulliver, the chief personality in Swift's *Gulliver's Travels,* visited the land of the Laputans. Living in an island in the sky, these highly intellectual people were preoccupied with the study of music and mathematics which caused them to be so introspective that they had profound difficulty in communicating with one another.

To cope with this situation the Laputans appointed special officers called "flappers." The task of the flapper was to facilitate communication by taking a stick with a balloon on it and touching the mouth of the person who wished to speak, and then touching the ear of the person who was to listen. "Those people who are able to afford it keep a flapper in their family," wrote Jonathan Swift.

In our modern families, the wife has inherited the task of the flapper. Some studies of patterns of conversation have shown that the stereotype of the talkative woman and the silent husband are not true and that the man speaks more often and for longer periods of time. But this may be due to women taking the "flapper role," for as Derber suggests, ". . . even when women talk it is often to steer attention to others rather than themselves."[2]

At the same time as Jonathan Swift was working on *Gulliver's Travels* and making his point about the flappers in the Laputan society, a woman in the Church of England rectory in Epworth, England, was displaying for everyone the possibilities of attention for developing the potentialities of her family. Her name was Susanna Wesley who gave birth to nineteen children, of whom ten grew to adulthood. She gave these children their elementary education, and the boys had only to go to preparatory school before proceeding to Oxford University. John became the founder of a world church, Charles the celebrated hymnwriter who composed over 5,000 hymns. Samuel was a scholarly priest of the Church of England, and one daughter, Martha, was a member of the inner circle of the famous lexicographer, Dr. Samuel Johnson.

The part played by attention in the development of this family is seen in a letter written by Susanna to John in which she told of her relationship with the children, "I take as much time as I can spare every night to talk with each child apart. On Monday I talk with Molly; on Tuesday with Hetty; Wednesday with Nancy; Thursday with Jacky; Friday with Patty; Saturday with Charles; and Emily and Suky together on Sunday." One dramatization of the experience of the Wesley family tells of a letter from John as he struggled with a difficult situation, "Oh,

Mother, what I'd give for a Thursday evening."[3]

What Destroys a Family?

Almost everyone knows that the family is of vital importance for the life of the nation and much time is given to the discussion of the reasons for the lamentable deterioration of family life today. Although outsiders may be blamed, the parents are still held to be responsible. Their transgressions may include such matters as: mothers who work outside the home mainly for selfish reasons (many mothers *have* to for survival), irresponsible parents, cruel parents, failure to provide adequate food and clothing, dominant fathers who seek to fulfill their personal ambitions through the children's sports, sexually abusive parents, nagging mothers and fathers, parents who abuse alcohol and other drugs, and/or parents who indulge every whim of their children.

However, there may another explanation! The problem may lie in *nothing*. Family members may be guilty of ignoring their responsibility to give attention to their children and just do *nothing*. This is the worst form of attack on the family.

Blessed are the parents who realize that the family cannot afford to hire a flapper but set about to fulfill a similar role, setting the example by their attention to each other, and then training the members of the family to be attention-givers rather than attention-receivers.

Notes

1. Charles Derber, *The Pursuit of Attention* (Oxford University Press, 1979), 48.

2. Derber, 59.

3. *The Works of John Wesley* (Grand Rapids: Zondervan Publishing House, 1972), vol. 1, 386.

7

Holding the Attention of a Group

"Sometimes the manners of our people are inimical to attention; they attend the chapel but do not attend to the preacher."
—Charles Haddon Spurgeon

The book *Mein Kampf* (our struggle) became the basic document on which its author, Adolph Hitler, built the action program of the Nazi movement. In this volume, this "master" of handling groups of people (for the worst unfortunately), stated a philosophy of leadership, "The art of leadership consists in consolidating the attention of the people against a single adversary and taking care that nothing will split up the attention."

Anyone who appears before groups of people can tell about the difficulties involved in trying to communicate with them and the awful, constantly present possibilities of "splitting up the attention of the group." In this chapter, we are focusing on some of the techniques that can be used in catching or regaining the attention of a group of people.

Demanding the Attention of the Group

The old question is, "If a tree in the forest crashes to the ground and there is no one there to hear it, does it make a sound?" If we are talking in terms of communication theory the answer is no. There is no communication unless the transmitted sound is received by someone. A speaker to a group has every reason to be apprehensive, if her audience is not paying attention. If there is no attention, there will be no communication. The moment the speaker opens her mouth she enters into a contest with individuals who for some reason do not want to pay attention.

While traveling on an international airline flight, I noted the way the safety instructions were given. These instructions are of vital importance for the passengers, but few people bother to take much notice of what is being said. In an effort to overcome this lack of attention some airlines have resorted to using videos featuring two attractive flight attendants. The lights in the cabin are dimmed and the screen in the front of the cabin comes alive in an effort to "consolidate the attention."

On a recent flight, I encountered another attempt to get the passenger's attention. An authoritative voice came over the P.A. system, "Ladies and gentlemen, I must have your *complete attention* as I explain the safety features of this aircraft." They will be fortunate, if they ever get *complete attention*. However it is an attempt to demand attention.

Traveling on a coach tour of the beautiful country of New Zealand we started one morning with a new driver. He had greeted the group, and as was their custom, a little covey of the tourists were telling each other about the previous night's activities. Suddenly the guide in a petulant voice spoke over the P.A. system, "If you people at the back are going to continue to talk while I am speaking, I will have to stop." It did the trick, at least for a short period of time, but some of the folk said they felt like children being rebuked by their teacher. Perhaps it may have been because they were behaving like children with attention deficit disorder.

Your Most Effective Call for Attention May Be Wordless

For many years I have been speaking to youth on the subject of "Your Developing Love Life," in which I discuss love, sex, courtship, and marriage. Most of the parents are aware that their children need help in this area. The children are not always so sure. In almost every group there are one or two who sit with a look on their face that says in effect, "My parents are trying to make my decisions again—here I am; see what you can do."

I receive some interesting non-verbal feedback. A girl will sit with crossed legs kicking one foot up and down with a rather obvious message. A boy will be slipping one arm around the girl alongside him and sometimes a couple of kids will hold surreptitious conversations.

When this difficult situation develops, I have found that the most effective technique is simply to stop and not speak a word. In the awkward silence that follows, the culprits will generally quit and look at me with a guilty look on their faces, to which action I reply with, "Thank you very much." Silence is an effective way of handling such a situation.

Refuse to Accept Inattention

To me, it is a most frustrating experience to be at a gathering where someone stands to make a statement to a group where the people pay no attention and persist in continuing with their conversations. The would-be speaker struggles, getting nowhere. It is far better for the speaker to demand their attention. This can be done by stopping and making a polite request, "Ladies and gentlemen, please give me your attention," or to use one of a number of attention-demanding techniques, which we will discuss in this chapter.

Charles Haddon Spurgeon was the outstanding Victorian preacher possessed of a communication skill rarely seen before or since his time. Yet, even this remarkable speaker had his difficult moments. In a lecture to his students, he related how he handled it:

> They are not in the habit of attending. They attend the chapel but do not attend the preacher. They are accustomed to look around at everyone who enters the place, and they come in at all times, sometimes with much squeaking of boots and banging of doors. I was preaching once to a people who continually looked around, and I adopted the expedient of saying, "Now, friends, as it is very interesting to you to know who comes in, and it disturbs me so very much for you to look around, I will, if you like, describe each as he comes in, so that you may sit and look at me, and keep up at least a show of decency." I described one gentleman who came in, who happened to be a friend whom I could depict without offense, as "a very respectable gentleman who had just taken his hat off," and so on, and after that one attempt I found it was not necessary to describe any more."[1]

Let any speaker who struggles with the moments when the attention of his audience lags, take courage. Even the Prince of Preachers had a similar experience. Like Him, we need to adapt ourselves to the situation and regain the lost treasure of attention.

Two Types of Initiatives

The term *initiative* is used to mean any active assertion to gain or keep attention. Efforts to attract attention can be called *gaining initiatives* and includes moves to gain the floor or to introduce one's own topics. Efforts to hold attention once it is gotten, either by continuing to speak or prolonging one's topics, can be called *sustaining initiatives*. How much attention anyone receives is decided primarily by the frequency and persistence of both types of initiatives and their success in competition with others.[2]

The Relationship Between Group Positioning and Attention

The most famous of all sermons in the history of the novel is probably that recorded in Melville's book *Moby Dick*. Ishmael, about to embark on a whaler, attended church in the Whaleman's Chapel on Sunday morning. The rain was pouring, and Ishmael followed a time-honored practice of many churchgoers—in his words, "I seated myself near the door."

A preacher, sailor, and harpooner in his early days, he climbed the rope ladder to the pulpit shaped like the bow of a ship. He looked over what Melville described as his "scattered people" and ordered them to "condense" and shouted, "Starboard gangway, there! Side away to larboard—larboard gangway! Midships! Midships!"

How I envy that preacher! I have suffered so long at the hands of skittish churchgoers who insist on sitting in the backseats and compel the newcomers, generally visitors, to move into the seats in the front. While visiting a number of London theaters, I could not help but notice the way in which the seats at the front came right up to the stage. These were the most desirable seats for theatergoers, but apparently when people come to church, they see it differently. Proximity has a relationship to attention which may be stated as:

The Quality of Our Attention to Others Is Indicated by Our Proximity to Them

The closer we are to people the more we indicate our attention to them. The preacher in Whaleman's Chapel was calling on his "scattered" people to "condense" in the hope of getting them to pay closer attention to his sermon. Incidentally, the sermon was on the subject of the prophet Jonah and contained a warning that Jonah was running away, separating himself from God, who was seeking his attention.

Personal space has been defined as, " . . . the area individuals actively maintain around themselves into which others cannot intrude without arousing discomfort." Which reminds us of a psychologist of yesteryear who made a study of the way that people used space. He concluded that there were four categories of interpersonal space:

> *Intimate.*—From direct contact to between six and eighteen inches.
> *Personal.*—One and a half to two and a half feet. Good friends would be an example.
> *Social.*—Four to twelve feet. People at a social gathering would be an example.
> *Public.*—Twelve to fifteen feet. This is probably why being in a crowded elevator can be a threatening experience.

The latter would seem to be rather excessive, and it certainly does not apply to people sitting in a meeting. In that instance, it would be closer to the distance indicated in personal (One and a half to two and a half feet). One expert in conducting group experiences of interaction insists that the participants sit in a circle within which the chairs, if not the bodies, are physically touching.

One study has shown that when a wife complains about her husband being distant her statement might be literally true. The researcher took 108 couples and told them to walk towards each other until they reached a "comfortable conversation distance," and the distance was then measured. The couples were given tests that reveal marital intimacy, divorce potential, and desire for change. The results showed that the further husbands stood from their wives the greater their dissatisfaction with their marriage.[3]

Psychologists have used this concept in evaluating a

family unit and state it as, "When the family sits down, the family therapist should pay attention to how they position themselves. Often their placement can give him some hunches about family affiliation." The would-be communicator who looks down upon his family-audience and sees them scattered to the four winds gets some hunches that are not too encouraging.

Split Audience—Split Attention

The problems is: How can we avoid the split attention of an audience, when the audience itself is physically split? Pity the speaker in a typical situation at a banquet where the caterers have scattered the round tables into every remote corner of the hall or the conference room where the delegates loll on the backseats and look as if they are about to drift to sleep.

I have frequently lamented the shape of church auditoriums and advocated some of the shapes—like fans, for example—that we are seeing today. A visit to Epcot at Walt Disney World was a revelation to me and opened up another possibility. In some of the exhibits the visitors take their place in mobile chairs that move in close to the display and then proceed on to the next highlight. How I wish that some mechanical genius would design a device for churches so that people entering at the back of the auditorium would take their seats and then be moved forward to give to and receive the attention of the preacher. Until that day comes, the speaker will do everything he can to get as close to the people whose attention he seeks.

As you look over your audience, it may be divided into areas of terms of the attention they are paying—the children who are drawing on paper, sleeping, or teasing their siblings or friends, the adolescents who are furtively trying to communicate with each other, and the adults who are weary and bored. As the little poem puts it:

> I never see my preacher's eyes,
> No matter how bright they shine,
> When he prays he shuts them tight,
> When he preaches, he closes mine!

Then there are those wonderful people who sit looking up with bright and eager eyes who will give their encouraging attention to the speaker.

This mentioning of eyes reminds us that the speaker who wants the attention of his audience must first of all give his own attention to them. Charles Osgood, the outstanding radio and television personality, writing about public speaking tells of a way to gain eye contact,

> There are too many people to establish eye contact with. OK, don't try. Just pick out three friendly faces. One left, one right, one center . . . By speaking first to one, then to the other, you take in the whole audience. Everybody perceives you to be looking in their direction at least a third of the time. Nobody feels neglected.
>   Look at the audience—the audience is king
>   Don't look at the microphone. It cannot see a thing.[4]

As we will later notice the beginning of an attention experience is looking. Eye contact is vital—people expect to be looked at.

Getting the Audience in Place

Positioning, as a factor in group attention, follows looking. Carol Burnett tells of her experience as a college student when she took a job as an usher at Warner Brother's Theater in Hollywood. The manager had developed a series of hand signals showing where he wanted the patrons to be seated.

> . . . he'd make a gun signal with his thumb and index finger. It meant "shoot." (It reminded me of when Homay and I used to play Lone Ranger.) I'd wait for the second half, which could be a finger or two, telling which aisle to "shoot" the customers to. If he wanted to shoot them to balcony, instead of, or in addition, an

aisle, he'd turn his palm, down this time and put his index up to touch the middle of his hand. Balcony. Yessirree.[5]

All of this hoopla went on to get the audience in the approved portion of the theater where the communication was being done mechanically. How much more important is placing the congregation in a situation where there is so much interaction between speaker and audience. Despite this factor, the ushering in church is generally done in a cursory offhand manner.

What is the most inattentive portion of any audience? Simple; the empty chairs. A close-knit audience with few empty chairs gives a speaker a special sense of his hearer's attentiveness.

The Processes of Group Interaction

One snowy January day we drove across Illinois to Missouri to fulfill an engagement in a church. As we slid along the icy roads, I inwardly speculated there would be few people in attendance. But I had underestimated those hardy Missourians. The fellowship hall was packed with people. As I sat on the platform and looked at that sea of eager faces, all eyes on me, all the tiredness of the difficult drive disappeared. I could hardly wait to make my presentation, and when the chairman made what I considered to be an overlong introduction, I had to fight the temptation to jump and push him out of the way. As I stood before those eager eyes of the compacted crowd, the words came tumbling from my lips. They roared at my jokes, and the whole meeting took a joyous note. The compact attentive group made all the difference.

There was another plus in this situation. The compact group affected one another. The use of humor gives us an excellent example. Humor is a process of interchange between the speaker and the audience. Humor skillfully used leads to a series of beneficial interactions from speaker to audience and within the audience.

The raconteur begins by creating or thinking about an anecdote and deciding to tell it. In delivering his story, he carefully builds the setting, creating uncertainty and curiosity as to the outcome. His audience rewards him with the greatest of all gifts—attention. At the appropriate moment (referred to as timing by the professionals), the raconteur delivers his punch line, which causes the audience to demonstrate their attention by laughing, and in this interaction of the group, their suggestibility is raised. This attentive response gives the raconteur an ego boost. He recalls or creates another anecdote—and the cycle begins again.

Dick Sheppard, the noted Anglican preacher, served briefly at the historic Saint Paul's Cathedral, but his biographer notes, "Sheppard was not at his best in a pulpit like St. Paul's where the speaker was remote from his hearers; he was most effective in a hall where the audience and the speaker were close together." Proximity promotes attention.

Recapturing that Lost Prize

The relationship between a speaker and his audience can be likened to a love affair. It begins with the time-honored formula (boy meets girl); speaker meets audience. The speaker must impress the audience and win their attention. He can do this in various ways such as responding to an introduction. A faculty member introduced at considerable length a friend of his to an audience. When the speaker commenced, he said, "Thank you so much for that gracious introduction, I could listen to an introduction like that all the morning, and for a moment I thought I was going to have to." He had their attention.

Because attention is mobile, a speech goes through a

number of phases. Like the love affair in which, after the initial attraction, the relationship may become routine and on occasions deteriorate to moments of antagonism, there are moments when the listener's interest drags, and his attention is lost. Some authorities claim that there is one serious lapse of attention in a auditor every seven minutes. I feel the average attention span may be shorter than this. The situation requires that the speaker like the lover must be prepared to recapture the elusive attention by periodically wooing his audience as he goes along.

Good Speaking Is One-Fourth Preparation and Three-Fourths Theater

Sam Johnson stands behind the podium at the head table. He has been introduced as the associate editor of the *Times Herald*, and he is about to address the annual banquet of the employees and families of Acton House Publishing Company. Sam briefly thanks the chairman, pauses, and says, "Sir Winston Churchill once said about his work as an author, 'Writing a book was an adventure. To begin with it was a toy, an amusement, then it became a mistress, and then a master, and then a tyrant and then I fling it to the public.' We are in the business of flinging books to the public and it isn't always easy."

The audience is his. The apt quotation and application are rewarded as they give him their attention, but as he continues to make his presentation, he is confronted with his first test in the improbable form of Mr. Harrison, treasurer of Acton House. Mr. Harrison, now a late arrival, has been delayed by an unfortunate accident of the freeway where he was obliged to stop to see if he could help. He is accompanied by his wife and their neighbors Mr. and Mrs. Miller. The party moves as quickly as they can to their position at the head table. Sam's contest is on as a ripple runs over the audience, and explanations are whispered as to the identify of the group.

The speaker, vividly aware that the new arrivals have captured his audience's attention, nods a greeting in the party's direction and raises his voice to declare, "We must not only spread information we must (raises his voice) *trumpet it from the housetops . . .* " and has the satisfaction of seeing the faces of most of the delinquent listeners as they look in his direction. But not for long.

Ian Marsh, headwaiter of the hotel, knows how much the manager of the hotel prizes the Acton House account and begins to speculate inwardly that Mr. Harrison's party might faint from hunger. He recalls too that the treasurer will sign the check for the catering bill and hopefully add a gratuity. So he tiptoes down to the newly seated treasurer and his friends and begins to move around their group, inquiring as to whether he should bring them a meal, only to be told they will eat later but would appreciate a cup of coffee. This whispering and consulting does nothing to help Sam's presentation.

Sam regroups and applies his energies to pulling his audience back to him,

> We are talking tonight about the use of words in our publishing activities. Many of these words have a similar sound but may have a different meaning. A man in Florida went scuba diving in search of treasure that might be on the sea bottom. After diving all the afternoon without success, he swam into the beach. Walking up out of the ankle-depth water, he kicked a gold doubloon, which goes to show, *booty is sometimes only shin deep.*

The roar of laughter gives Sam a warm feeling, but unfortunately another type of warm feeling is bothering some women in the audience. Some of the women had earlier complained about the air conditioning being too cold and a waiter turned down the thermostat, now they felt it was too hot. One woman picked up the printed program and began to fan herself, and every overheated female in sight got the message. Despite his resolution to ignore the waving fans, Sam begins to feel that the women are waving him good-bye, and he resolves to make a new effort at retrieval.

Sam says, "Let me remind you that words on paper have always been important—the pen is mightier than the sword. As one poet has said it, 'We must be free or die who speak the tongue that Shakespeare spake, the faith and morals hold that Milton held.'" Sam's friend Wayman Harris led the applause.

Mention of Shakespeare has touched the heart of Dr. Stanley Smith, an English teacher from Clifford College, and he leans forward in a huddle with his friends around the table and reminds them of what Bradley said about Shakespeare's use of the word *freedom*. Sam mentally speculates as to whether this group is a part of his audience or a football team going into a huddle. He stops speaking and raises his glass of water to his lips, all the while gazing intently at the huddlers who soon become aware of his stare, begin to look embarrassed, and turn eager eyes to the speaker.

Sam is underway again and doing well until he runs into those inhabitants of the banquet table who indulge themselves with iced tea. The accomplished iced tea drinker periodically shakes his glass. The purpose—mixing up the lemon and sugar to an ideal consistency, but it has an unfortunate effect on the human ear and everybody within twenty feet can hear the sound of ice blocks on glass. This sound of the tea glass rattler is guaranteed to divert the attention of any listener.

Taking his clue from the problem, Sam takes up with the problem of drunk driving, resorts to his water glass which he holds high, and invites his listeners to see this as representing a glass of liquor. He paints the picture of a man attending a party who approaches the glass, has his fill, and then comes from the other side to go out and drive down the highway to an accident with awful results which are graphically portrayed by the speaker.

He has them back in the hollow of his hand, but there is a new challenge as Jerry Crump, who had indulged himself at the earlier "happy hour," has drifted off into a deep sleep, punctuated with a periodic snore, much to the amusement of the people who are sitting around. As the situation deteriorates, two families feel they have to get on home and begin to move out. Sam rescues this latter situation by saying, "This reminds me of a movie I once saw in which a play is opening and will shortly be closing on Broadway, and the commentator remarks, 'The plot thickens, the audience thins.' "

And so it goes on, beepers, babies crying, children running out to the bathroom. It is a contest which calls for all the resources of the speaker to capture that elusive commodity called attention.

An Expert's Counsel

Charles Haddon Spurgeon was one of the greatest orators the church has ever produced. He gave lectures to his students which contained many important principles. One lecture on the subject of "attention" has some relevant statements. A sampling of these follows:

• "It may be their duty to attend but it is far more your duty to make them do so. The minister who recommended the old lady to use snuff in order to keep from dozing was very properly rebuked by her reply—that if he would put more snuff into the sermon she would be awake enough."

• "Frequently it is very difficult for congregations to attend, because of the place and atmosphere. The next best thing to the grace of God for a preacher is oxygen."

• "Sometimes the manners of our people are inimical

to attention; they attend the chapel but do not attend to the preacher."

- "In order to get attention, the first golden rule is, always say something worth saying, and let this good matter be clearly arranged."

- "Make your manner as pleasing as it can possibly be. Do not indulge in monotones. Do vary your voice continually."

- "Avoid being too long. An old preacher said to his young friend, 'I do not care what else you preach about, but I wish you would always preach about forty-five minutes.' " (author's note: How times have changed!)

- "There should be a goodly number of illustrations in our discourses . . . most of the greatest preachers have abounded in similes, metaphors, allegories, and anecdotes."

- "Cultivate the surprise element. Do not say what everybody expected you would say."

Communicating with a group of people is one of the most exciting experiences of a human being,if he has their attention. Carol Burnett tells of one of her earliest efforts at acting while a student at UCLA. On the opening night of a comedy about a "mountain family," she was nervous but went on stage with the walk and accent of people she had known in her Texas childhood, and received a tremendous response. She describes her experience, "When I exited into the wings of wait for the next cue, I had the funniest feeling that the audience had *come off stage with me*, they *hadn't wanted me to leave*, and I wasn't nervous anymore, just excited and feeling wanted."[6]

The joy of seeing your audience expectantly eager and anxious to hear what you have to say is a marvelous experience of feeling them responding to what you are saying. In Carol's words, "Coming off stage with you." These are products of the quality of the attention which they pay. If you do not have the ability to demand this attention, the experience can be frustrating and depressing. Time spent in learning techniques of gaining and holding attention will be amply rewarded, as we learn to transform frustration to elation in the joy of effective, dynamic verbal communication.

Notes

1. Charles Haddon Spurgeon, *Lectures to My Students*.
2. Derber, 14.
3. "Mind Openers," *Psychology Today*, vol. 22, No. 3, March 1988, 14.
4. Charles Osgood, "Osgood on Speaking," *American Way*, August 1988, 26.
5. Carol Burnett, *One More Time* (New York: Random House, 1986), 176.
6. Ibid., 173.

8

Developing the Craft as an Attention Giver

"It has capabilities, my Lord."
—*Capability Brown*

My concern with the assimilative processes of communication came from a longtime interest in the subject of communication. The subject of listening became a focal point for me as I wrote articles, two books, and delivered numerous lectures and talks on the listening theme. I was involved in this study for a considerable time, before it dawned on me that much of the writing about listening was really a discussion of the subject of attention without a clear distinction between the receiving and giving aspects of attention.

One of my aims in this book is to clarify what is involved in the attending experiences and to show that any attempt to limit attending experiences to listening will be mistaken. Listening is obviously the best known of the attending experiences, but it is only *one* of a number of attending techniques that can be used, which include such experiences as looking, questioning, touching, and praising. In the chapters of the book that follow, we will focus on these skills.

Create an Attention Habit

The story is told of the British army veteran, who was retired and living in an apartment. Each day at noon he walked down the stairs across a square to a restaurant where he took delivery of his midday meal. He carried his food on a tray across the square and up to his apartment, and a fellow ex-soldier observing him decided to take advantage of habits built by years of training. As the veteran walked across the square holding a food-laden tray in front of him, his friend shouted the most-used command in the army, "attention." The response was predictable as the veteran snapped to attention, arms by his side, and lunch on the street.

By linking attention to a habit reminds us of the frequently overlooked power of habits that people have. Common use of the word *habit* has associated the word with "bad habits" more often than it has with "good habits." We need to remember that we are not only "creatures" of habits, but we can be the "creators" of habits just as well.

The Rules of Habit Formation

(1) Decide on your habit objective of constantly being "on task" and paying attention.

(2) Launch into your attention-giving activity with abandon.

(3) Don't allow a single exception until the habit is established.

(4) Keep your attention-giving habit alive by constant daily activity.

There is no sense on working on building a habit that is not going to be of value to you in some important aspect of your life. The Duke of Wellington was not only the victor over Napoleon Bonaparte at the Battle of Waterloo, but he was also one of the great personalities of the Victorian era. His insistence on excellence in the British army led to the use of a phrase popular among the troops for many years after his death. If some work was done and any doubt remained about its quality, they would say, "It wouldn't have done the Duke." This phrase referred to the standards that the Duke insisted upon having

When the Duke reviewed the use of drill in army training practices he said, "Habit second nature? Habit is ten times nature."

If this statement is true, we may need to remind ourselves that learning attention skills will influence every area of life including, as we will later see, our relationship to God, friends and family. It will be a worthy skill for habit formation.

The redoubtable William James liked to use a metaphor by saying that habits are the flywheel of society. A flywheel is an important part of many machines. Once the machine is moving the flywheel provides the momentum that keeps it moving.

As a boy, I had the responsibility for starting a one-cylinder internal combustion engine by winding a strap around the large external flywheel. I tugged and tugged with that strap, while the green monster huffed and puffed, coughed and spluttered. Then it sprang to life with a splutter and gave a hum that was music to my ears. The green monster had ample power and would hum away all day; all it needed was the special effort to get moving and the momentum of the flywheel kept it moving. Habits are just like the flywheel that keeps us going.

Start by reading the latter half of this book from chapter 10 on and then focus on the five basic activities that are described.

- Begin with the basic activity of *looking*. When you

meet another person, look them in the eye. Don't stare them down—practice the skill of giving them a gentle coaxing visual caress.

• Incorporate your looking skills into *learning to listen*, following the processes recommended in the chapter on the art of listening. Remember it is an art and recall the hours of practice put in by the musician, ballet dancer, or artist.

• Questioning is a rare skill that can be developed. Be particularly careful to avoid the pitfalls mentioned in chapter 12.

• Learn the techniques of touch. Watch out for the ways you use these skills, particularly with people of the opposite sex. Children, older people, and lonely people all need hugs.

• Develop your praise power with the recognition that praise is the highest form of attention.

When William James pointed out the way in which certain activities are painstakingly learned and then automatically carried on, he said the important goal is, "To make our nervous system our ally instead of our enemy." The small unit of the nervous system is the neuron. These neurons are linked by synaptic connections, tiny gaps over which the neural current must jump as it moves the message to the appropriate destination. The more frequent the neural current jumps the gap the easier the subsequent journeys. Thus, a neuron memory, which is part of our nervous system, is built and enables us to automatically carry on the activities learned with difficulty.

There is a sense in which our nervous system is like a computer. The computer has tremendous power, but it must be programmed. The same is true of our neural system; it is powerful and can be programmed. The surest way of programming it is by constant repetition, not allowing a single exception.

Few men changed the face of England in the way that Capability Brown did. Living in the eighteenth century, when a man's station in life was determined by the family he was born into, Brown started life as a gardener. He had remarkable native gifts of landscaping architecture and worked his way up until he was sought by the nobility of England to design the landscaping of their magnificent ornate country residences, and he became gardener to the king as well. He was so widely involved in these enterprises that when he was invited to visit Ireland he responded that he couldn't come because, "I have not finished England yet."

Blenheim Palace was the gift of a grateful nation to John Churchill for his services in winning the Battle of Blenheim. Incidently, this was the place of Winston Churchill's inadvertent birth. The magnificent lands surrounding the palace were the work of Brown. His achievements were so wide that he was called, "Nature's second husband," and it was confidently asserted that when he died he would go on to remodel heaven.

Capability Brown's name came from his attitude toward his work. Upon being shown a vast area of land surrounding an ornate house, he would respond to a question as to what he could do. His response was often, "It has capabilities, my Lord." He saw his task to see possibilities in landscapes. Our task is to see possibilities in people. Whenever we meet someone, we should say that, "This person has capabilities." We can help develop these capabilities by the skillful use of our powers of attention.

Assimilative and expressive attentional skills are not easy to acquire and most of us need instruction and practice in developing them. But take courage with practice and perseverance that mental muscle attention can be developed.

Part 2:

Five Levels
of Attention Giving

Praising

Touching

Concerned Questioning

Listening

Looking

9

Using the Basic Skill of Looking

"The Lord turned and looked straight at Peter"
(Luke 22:61, NIV).

Focused attention starts with looking. Spurgeon stated on one occasion, "I often talk with my eyes to the orphan boys at the foot of my pulpit. We want all eyes fixed upon us and all eyes open to us. To me it is an annoyance if even a blind man does not look at me with his face."[1]

The attention-giver must look the part, and he begins by looking. Ralph Waldo Emerson once noted, "The eyes of men converse as much as their tongues, with the advantage that the ocular needs no dictionary, but is understood the world over."

In the New Testament, there are many illustrations of communication, but none is more impressive than the example of nonverbal communication at the trial of Jesus. Peter, His disciple, had freely affirmed his loyalty, but Jesus had warned His disciple that he would deny his Lord three times. At the trial Peter was standing near the soldiers. Three times people came by and challenged the disciple, but he denied any knowledge of Jesus. Then as His Master had predicted, the rooster crowed. The record tells us, "The Lord turned and looked straight at Peter.

113

Then Peter remembered" (Luke 22:61, NIV). The look had carried an eloquent message.

Looking at the person on whom we focus attention, we not only create an impression on them, but we learn something. How is this person dressed—neatly or untidily; expensively or cheaply; modestly or in a showy fashion? What is the general demeanor of this person—confident, tentative, belligerent, deferential? How does he sit—upright, tensely, with both feet on the ground, slouched, with legs crossed? What mood do his eyes convey—furtiveness, apprehensiveness, concentration, or abject sadness?

When a group of people sit to talk together, there should, ideally, be a tacit agreement that the group members will take turns at talking. We noted earlier that in focused attention there is a face-to-face contact which is like the act of the photographer, as he looks into the viewfinder of his camera and adjusts the focusing mechanism until the image is sharp and says nonverbally to his subject, "I am concentrating on you."

In a group conversation, each participant has three rights: (1) The right to complete a sentence or a brief thought; (2) The right to expect that the group will not blatantly ignore his or her interests, ideas, or reactions; and (3) The right to receive eye contact from the other members of the group. The latter is of fundamental importance.

Nothing is more disconcerting for me than to try to carry on a conversation with someone who is wearing dark glasses. Like the soldiers who were ordered not to fire their weapons until they saw the whites of their enemies' eyes, I feel that if I am going to have conversation with a person, I need to see the whites of his eyes. On occasion, I have said to clients who sat looking at the floor, "Look at me. I want to see your eyes." I want to indicate my attention by looking at them, and I want their response with eye contact.

The Power of the Smile

There are different ways of looking. One is a smile which has been called a "social display." A German ethologist has shown that smiling is about the closest thing we have to a universal characteristic in humankind. It is predictable that at about three months of age the human baby will smile. If an adult, the mother, gives social stimulation the baby will respond. Many mothers report that they now realize that they "are no longer the attendant of a screeching, diaper-soiling device but people involved in an intimate relationship,"[2] and in this experience they are dealing with another human being.

These developmental processes may be what has made humans so susceptible to the smile and anyone who hopes to influence another should know the power of the smile. During 1968-73, Henry Kissinger representing the U.S. negotiated with Xuan Thuy of North Vietnam in an effort to find a conclusion to the Vietnam debacle. Kissinger discovered that unlike the stereotype of the stoic poker-faced Oriental, his opposite member had a formidable weapon, ". . . he was tiny with a Buddha face, a sharp mind, perpetually smiling face while saying the most outrageous things." The smile was an effective instrument in the psychological conflict in which they were involved.

The smile has a special significance in interpersonal relations. A famous salesman of yesteryear, Frank Bettinger, wrote a book of which the great motivator Dale Carnegie said, "I can recommend it with enthusiasm . . . when I started to sell I would gladly have walked from Chicago to New York to get a copy of this book, if it had been available."[3]

Bettinger tells us that he had a handicap as a salesperson, "I had the sourest puss you ever gazed upon and I even have pictures to prove it . . . I soon discovered that a worried sour expression brought results that were just about infallible—an unwelcome audience and failure."

Bettinger decided to enter a program to change this.

> Each morning during my fifteen-minute bath and vigorous rubdown I determined to cultivate a big, happy smile, just for the fifteen minutes. It wasn't easy, the old worried face would come back again . . . so I'd force the smile. Back came cheerful, optimistic thoughts.
>
> "Although I didn't realize it until later, this experience seems to substantiate the theory of that great philosopher and teacher, Professor William James of Harvard. James said, "Action seems to follow feeling, but really action and feeling go together; and by regulating the action, which is under the direct control of the will, we can indirectly regulate the feeling, which is not."[4]

Wanted: A Few Smiling Faces

That heading was given in a help wanted ad for Mazio's Pizza. "Thus the sovereign voluntary pathway to cheerfulness, if our cheerfulness be lost, is to sit up cheerfully and to speak and act as if cheerfulness is already there. . . ."[5]

While I was taping a series of TV programs, during one those apparently inevitable delays in the taping, a warning message came from the director through the floor manager, "Lighten up, Dr. Drakeford."

I suddenly realized what my wife has often told me, that I frequently lapse into a brown mood in which my face takes on a bored, uninterested appearance. If I am not on the alert and keep on working at it, I soon lose that important smiling face. Bettinger attacked this problem by instituting a program of asking people to pledge themselves to smile their happiest smile at every living creature they saw just for *thirty days*. He reports some of the wonderful results that came from the commitments.

Wouldn't this be a great idea for each of us to try?

Some years ago, a department store in New York recognized the pressure under which its salesclerks labored at Christmas and displayed the following:

The Value of a Smile at Christmas
It costs nothing but creates much.

It enriches those who receive, without impoverishing those who give.

It happens in a flash and the memory of it lasts forever.

None are so rich they can get along without it, and none so poor but are richer for its benefits.

It creates happiness in the home, fosters goodwill in a business, and is the countersign of friends.

It is rest to the weary, daylight to the discouraged, sunshine to the sad, and nature's best antidote for trouble.

Yet it cannot be bought, begged, borrowed, or stolen, for it is something that is no earthly good to anybody until it is given away.

And if in the last-minute rush of Christmas buying, some of our salespeople should be too tired to give you a smile, may we ask you to leave one of yours?

For nobody needs a smile so much as those who have none left to give.

The Chinese have a saying, "A man without a smiling face should not open a shop." A smile is an equally indispensable weapon in the attention giver's armament.

> The loveliest thing the lady wore
> Was nothing purchased in a store.
> Yet all about her noticed it
> And marveled at the perfect fit.
> Though worn for years 'twas ever new
> And sparkled like the morning dew.
> It added charm to changing style;
> Perhaps you've guessed—it was a SMILE.

Facial Feedback

Most of us know how important our looks are, but we don't take pains to discover how we look and then swing into action to do something about it. I once met a man who was an engineer and a genius at mathematics. When I told him my son's birthdate, he responded, "That would be on a Monday." It so happened that he was looking at one of my books in which there were six simple outline drawings of faces. As he looked at one with the inscription *boredom*, his wife said to him, "That's the way you generally look."

He was startled and replied, "I never realized that before. I must do something about it." His response proved he was really intelligent.

One of the most telling aspects of looking may be the deliberate wink. Mrs. Harrison, a woman of middle years who has succeeded in remaining youthful despite difficult years in a foreign country, specializes, of all things, in the wink—not a flirtatious wink, but a gentle lowering of the top eyelid to join its companion, saying in effect, "You are right—dead right!"

This wink is so effective that when she sits in one of my classes during a lecture I find my eye moving in her direction in search of reinforcement. In fact, I find it difficult to resist the urge to reply in the same manner, but I do resist, in order to save myself from the accusation that I am carrying on a classroom flirtation with a missionary! Mrs. Harrison is an expert in using looking as a technique of giving attention.

Any speaker worthy of his calling will have to learn the value of the look. Jonathan Edwards, the Puritan preacher, was said to have special power in his look. ". . . his wasted form and thin voice suggestive of a being come from the gates of death, and his eye, when it was lifted so piercing that it was profanely said on one occasion that it 'looked off' the bell rope in the steeple, so that the bell fell with a crash into the church."[6] The exaggerated report is evidence of the potent look of Edwards.

The look of attention may have therapeutic value. A psychologist told of a depressed client who had decided to end it all by driving down the freeway to a familiar spot where there was a large concrete abutment and steer his automobile into it. Stopped by a red light at the on ramp, he looked over at the driver in the lane alongside him. She was a particularly attractive young woman. As he was looking at her, she chanced to look in his direction and gave him a friendly smile to which he responded with a similar smile. The light changed and her car drew rapidly ahead. As he drove down the freeway toward the abutment, he found himself thinking about the congenial young woman and the sweet smile and concluded that if a pretty woman could take time to give him a friendly greeting, life wasn't so bad after all, and he drove off the freeway at the next exit.

Probably no man has influenced the study of personality, for better or for worse, more than did Sigmund Freud, the famous Viennese psychiatrist. Founder of psychoanalysis, he was not impressive physically, being a modest five feet, seven inches tall, and conservatively dressed. The feature that caught the attention of observers was his penetrating stare. One colleague noted, " . . . the forward thrust of his head and critical exploring gaze of his keenly piercing eyes."[7] Looking is a rather obvious factor in the activities of the great investigator of the nature of personality, but it will be an even more important factor for the person interested in utilizing an attention technique for influencing personality.

A professor of speech at a large university was invited to speak at the graduation exercises of a country high school. It was not an easy assignment. As he stood before them to speak, he realized the people had come to see their children receive their diplomas and were not interested in a speech. The people in the audience talked with each other, as their small children ran up and down the aisles. As the speaker struggled with his speech, he had the feeling that as a professor of speech this was one of the greatest challenges he had ever faced. So he tried some special "tricks;" he raised his voice and shouted, no difference in response. He lowered his voice to a whisper, no response. He walked to the front of the platform, no response. He told a funny story, still no response. Then he remembered one last desperate idea. Was anyone listening? He ran his eyes over the audience and saw one bearded, elderly man looking up, nodding his head, obviously the only intent listener in the audience. So the professor narrowed his range of eye contact and focused on the elderly gentlemen who kept nodding responses.

Following the conclusion of the graduation the school superintendent escorted the professor to the social hall for a cup of coffee and as they drank the superintendent said, "Would you like to meet some of these people?"

The professor not impressed with this audience said, "No, I don't think I really need to meet any of them." Then he espied his solitary listener, "I'd like to meet that elderly gentlemen with the beard."

"All right," replied the superintendent, "I'll do that. It may be difficult. He's stone deaf."

The important thing was that the elderly gentleman *looked* as if he were listening. The look had saved the professor's day.

Sometimes the way we look denies what we say. I once went to hear a lecture by a famous sociologist. He turned out to be a congenial fellow, who, following his lecture, gathered us around him as a group and said he wanted some feedback and wished to hear what we thought on the subject.

The sociologist's reactions to the people who spoke were a fascinating study in themselves. He turned his black eyes on the somewhat verbose questioner with a beady stare as if to lull him into a hypnotic trance and, hopefully, silence. If a participant persisted, the sociologist's bushy eyebrows began a rhythmic movement like two gyrating caterpillars poking faces at each other. His rather large red lips mouthed unspoken words, occasionally reinforced by strange incoherent sounds. Ham-like hands reached out in mesmeric movements.

When he spoke it was, "Go on," but the way he looked said clearly and unequivocally, "Keep quiet and let me talk."

In Charles Dickens's book, *Nicholas Nickleby,* the author gives us a picture of the archvillain Wackford Squeers. "Mr. Squeers's appearance was not prepossessing. He had but one eye, and the popular prejudice runs in favor of two. The eye he had was unquestionably useful, but decidedly not ornamental, being of a greenish grey, and in the shape of the fanlight of a street door. The blank side of his face was wrinkled and puckered up, which gave him a sinister appearance, especially when he smiled, at which times his expression bordered on the villainous."[8]

As an attention-giver, Squeers was a complete failure. The way he looked was against him. His attention would have been in the negative mode. The way Squeers looks, prepares for the villainous role he is to play in the novel. If I am to become an effective attention-giver, I must be aware that looking is the first level of attention-giving. Considering the way I look is the beginning step in this important process.

Notes

1. Davis Otis Fuller, *Spurgeon's Lectures to His Students* (Grand Rapids: Zondervan Publishing House, 1945), 104.

2. Melvin Konner, "The Enigmatic Smile," *Psychology Today,* March 1987, 44.

3. Frank Bettinger, *How I Raised Myself from Failure to Success in Selling* (New York: Simon & Schuster, 1982), iv.

4. Ibid., 100.

5. Dale Carnegie, *How to Win Friends and Influence People* (New York: Simon and Schuster, 1981), 99.

6. T. Harwood Pattison, *The History of Christian Preaching* (Philadelphia: American Baptist Publishing Society, 1903), 357

7. "A Piece of the True Couch," *Time*, April 18, 1988, 85.

8. "Charles Dickens, *Nicholas Nickleby*, (New York: Penguin Books, 1978), 90.

10

Developing
the Art of Listening

The Awesome Power of the Listening Ear
—Book title

Probably the best known of all attending skills is the skill of listening. In many instances people use the word *listening* when they could have used the word *attention*. Because of this, it will be important for us to clarify just what we mean by listening and note some of the things that listening is not. However, we must acknowledge that listening is easily the most important attending skill. We will do this by considering a number of propositions for an acrostic on the word *listen*.

Learn the truth about listening.
Investigate the difference between hearing and listening.
Show your interest in every way you know.
Tame unruly emotions.
Eliminate side excursions.
Never interrupt.

Learn the Truth About Listening

There's a good chance that when you note this chapter is about listening you will ask, "So what? Everybody knows about listening—the same old stuff." Because of this, we will consider some of the myths about listening and follow with the reality.

Myth 1.—Intelligent people are good listeners.

Reality.—It is often maintained that high-intelligence people automatically listen and comprehend well, because high-intelligence people generally have a great deal of ego strength, they frequently feel there is no need to study the listening skills. There is no evidence to show that this is so.

Intelligence may actually hinder listening. The highly intelligent person often becomes impatient with a slower-speaking individual, because he can't be bothered waiting for him to complete his statement and tunes him out.

Listening skills, like any other must be learned, practiced, and developed—regardless of intelligence level.

Myth 2.—Good hearing means good listening.

Reality.—Since listening is often confused with hearing, it is assumed hearing problems are the reason some people don't listen. However, investigation shows that many with perfectly good hearing are poor listeners.

What we do with our hearing equipment is an important consideration. Excellent equipment can be used for the wrong purpose, and good hearers can be poor listeners.

Myth 3.—Everyday listening builds the skill.

Reality.—We may learn to listen the way we learn to walk, but some children don't even learn to walk properly and need correction. Listening practice does not always make perfect—it is possible to practice our mistakes.

Myth 4.—Reading develops our listening ability.

Reality.—There are considerable differences between reading and listening. At its best, reading is a solitary experience, concentrating on a book. It may even foster an antisocial attitude. In contrast, listening is a social experience involving at least two people.

Dismiss these fallacies and realize that listening is a complex process and proceed to learn and understand the nature of this complex activity.

Investigate the Difference Between Hearing and Listening

Hearing and listening are not synonyms. The word *hear* describes the process whereby a sound comes through the air to your ear where it is changed to neural current and transmitted to the brain. The word *listening* is used for the process, whereby we sort the messages and decide which stimulus will have our attention.

The whole operation of a sound wave's transmission to the brain takes place at lightning speed. The brain itself is programmed by years of experience and conditioning to handle the auditory impressions it is fed. Like a busy executive's efficient secretary who sorts out the correspondence, keeping only the most important for his personal perusal, some sounds are summarily rejected, while others have total attention focused on them. This selective process of the brain is the main distinction between hearing and listening.

We live in a world today that is afflicted with pollution. But one type of pollution is not frequently mentioned—it is noise pollution.

Show Your Interest Every Way You Know How

Total listening might be described as the activity in which the listener goes to work to utilize every part of his body—his mouth, eyes, and so forth—to make the other person feel loved, valued, and worthwhile.

Frank Capra, the celebrated movie producer, spent some time with Franklin D. Roosevelt, at that time President of the United States, and described the way FDR entered into a conversation with him:

. . . with a big friendly smile, and the glint of interest in his sparkling eyes, he would encourage you to talk about yourself, your family, your work, anything.

"Well, I declare!" he'd exclaim after you'd made some inane statement. By little laughs, and goads, and urgings such as, "Really? Tell me more!" . . . "Well what do you know!" . . . "Same thing's happened to me dozens of times!" . . . "Oh, that's fascinating!" . . . his warmth would change you from a stuttering Milquetoast to an articulate raconteur.

Small wonder President Roosevelt, the man of the people, was able to marshal the forces of democracy against the tyranny of the Axis powers. Like the President you can be an effective listener if you will show your interest in every way you know how.

Tame Unruly Emotional Reactions

As we listen to a person speaking to us, there are some emotionally toned words that touch some reactions which may cause us to cut the speaker off, and communication is ruptured.

Harry Fontain is hanging a picture for his wife. An industrious businessman, he is the despair of his mate when it comes to household chores. Today, to her infinite delight he has come home from work and announced his attention to "get this picture on the wall."

He holds the picture in a temporary position and awaits his wife's final word of approval.

"Just a bit too high, Honey. Mother always said you had high ideas."

Harry's interest in picture hanging evaporates. He labors through that little chore in a halfhearted manner. "Mother always said . . ." is like waving a red flag to a bull.

So many of us have emotional reactions to certain

words. When we hear them, red lights flash, and alarm bells clang. The very moment some Republicans hear *Democrat* or an industrialist hears *union*, or there comes to our ears a word or a concept about which we feel strongly the emotional reaction goes into action. The good listener fights back the emotional response. He needs time to understand the other person and see the full implication of what is being said.

Eliminate Side Excursions

One of the problems faced by a listener is to know what to do with his leftover time. While some speakers may verbalize approximately 125 words per minute, most of us can think about four times that speed. As the speaker presents his ideas, we easily move along and keep up with him. It is so simple that we have time on our hands and so we occasionally dart ahead or go on a side excursion. These side excursions are particularly damaging and may lead to our downfall as listeners.

As you sit in an audience listening to a speaker, you move along with him for a short period. Then a picture of your office flashes onto the screen of your mind, and you see the pile of work awaiting your attention. So you take a mental trip back to your place of toil, look over your correspondence, check up on your secretary, then rejoin the speaker.

A little later in the discourse, the golf course begins to beckon and off you go. You bask in the warm sun, admire the condition of the greens, and see the old cronies. You visualize the beautiful drive, the flawless putt, your opponent's dismay, and the concluding moment of triumph.

But on one of these journeys you stay away too long and when you return it is to discover the speaker has gotten so far ahead that there is no chance of catching him now. So you sink into a passive resignation to your horrible fate, put a fixed look on your face, and hope the speaker will soon tire and quit.

The good listener doesn't go on side excursions. He tries to anticipate where the speaker is going, and the moment he sees him going in a different direction, he rushes back and joins with him again. No side excursions.

Never Interrupt

Any conversation is carried on in a context, and it is often necessary to have some information about the events leading up to the experiences under discussion. Some background material gives meaning to what is being related. Nevertheless, there are people whose passion for correctness and detail will bog down any effort at conversation.

Listen to Sonya and Bryant Gilmore talking with a group of their friends. Bryant is telling of an unusual experience which befell the Gilmore family on their last vacation. Sonya's eyes are gleaming, as she too in her imagination recalls that remarkable adventure.

"We left about the middle of July," begins Bryant.

"Not really the middle, Honey," says his sweet wife. "It was actually the 27th . . ."

"Was it really? You know, I thought it was about the 15th or 16th; in fact, I remember that was the day Harry Jones borrowed the lawnmower . . ."

The story is half ruined already. The listener begins to wonder inwardly if the Gilmores will ever get away on the trip.

Having failed to settle the date, Mr. Gilmore, just a little red in the face, plunges into his story, with Mrs. Gilmore hovering around like a vulture looking for fresh opportunities for prey.

"We threw in our lines, and in no time flat the fish were almost jumping into the boat. Within twenty minutes had the biggest mess of fish. We must have had fifty fish on the string by the time we stopped," he said.

"Oh, Honey, you know there were only twenty to thirty-five," his wife corrected.

"Thirty-five! Why, I caught twenty-five myself, and Johnny and Jimmy must have landed another twenty-five between them," he cried.

Mrs. Gilmore gives a sigh and looks apologetically at the company, "That's my husband! Always multiplies the number by two to make it sound good."

So the conversation goes on with Mr. Gilmore's annoyance index rapidly rising. He finally glares at his wife and lapses into silence.

Mrs. Gilmore, having made sure that every minute detail is correct and now vaguely aware of her spouse's antagonism, finally decides to retire to the kitchen to prepare a snack.

What did it matter whether they left for their vacation on July 11, 16, or 27, or whether they caught twenty-nine or fifty fish? These were side issues of no importance to the auditors. By insisting on the minutiae, Mrs. Gilmore had annoyed and frustrated her husband, embarrassed the visitors, and generally cast a shadow on the evening. A good listener resists the temptation to interrupt.

I hate to admit it but having read all of this chapter and knowing about listening, you may still not be a competent listener. Charles Darwin tells of his impressions of Thomas Carlyle, the famous man of letters, who certainly knew all the extant theories about listening but had little success in practicing the art of listening. He recorded an event that long lived with him, "I remember a funny dinner at my brother's where among a few others were Babbage and Lyell, both of whom liked to talk. Carlyle, however, silenced everyone by haranguing during the whole dinner on the advantages of silence."[1]

Carlyle, the brilliant author with so much knowledge, had such a need for attention that he could not bring himself to practice the art of giving attention to other people. This is the constant struggle of practitioners of the listening skills.

As a psychologist, I am not a follower of Sigmund Freud. His theories do not appeal to me. However, I have discovered over and over again the skill of the psychotherapist lies not so much in his theory as in his personality; it might be frankly stated that the personality of the therapist *is* the skill. One man who met Sigmund Freud stated his impression,

> He struck me so forcibly that I shall never forget him. He had qualities I had never seen in any other man. Never had I seen such *concentrated attention*. His eyes were mild and genial. His voice was low and kind. His gestures were few. But the attention he gave me, his appreciation of what I said, even when I said it badly, was extraordinary. *You've no idea what it meant to be listened to like that.*[2]

Here was the secret of the psychotherapist—his capacity to use concentrated attention by listening.

Listening is such an important aspect of attention that the word *listening* is frequently used when we should employ the word *attention*. A closer examination reveals that listening is really one form of attention but it is the most frequently used technique of the attention process. If you would be a skillful *attention-giver*, you must learn to listen.

Notes

1. Charles Darwin, *The Autobiography of Charles Darwin* (New York: Macmillan, 1958), 112-13.

2. Dale Carnegie, *How to Win Friends and Influence People* (New York: Simon & Schuster, 1981), 122.

11

Trying Some Concerned Questioning

I keep six honest serving men
(They taught me all I knew);
*   Their names are What and Why and When*
And How and Where and Who.
                        —Rudyard Kipling

It has long been known that the question is valuable tool for the teacher. It is one of the primary instruments in religious education which has used the catechism defined in the dictionary as "An instructional summary of a religion in question and answer form." Jesus, the greatest of all teachers, constantly had a question on His lips, and if you watch a skilled teacher in action, you will be constantly impressed by her skillful use of the question.

Not so well known is the fact that the question is also an important part of the work of the psychologist or counselor. This has given rise to the following anecdote during a conversation at a party:

"Are you a psychologist?" the first man asked.

"Why do you ask?" the second man replied.

"You *are* a psychologist." the first man said.

In the course of a presentation, outstanding clergyman Dr. Charles Allen told the audience he had developed a marvelous new counseling technique. Allen was already known for the books he had written, such as *God's Psychiatry* and *Twelve Ways to Solve Your Problems,* and the thought of a new counseling technique caused his audience to listen even more intently.

Allen presented his counseling methodology in his own inimitable way. When someone came for counseling, he said, he would ask, "What seems to be your situation?" His counselee would then proceed to recount all the difficulties he was facing, sometimes taking considerable time.

When at last this recital was concluded, the astute clergyman would ask a second question: "What do you think you should do?" His client then advanced his ideas about the courses of action that had been presented, and the time had come to end the counseling session. Attention provoked by questioning had done the trick. The questioning technique is also used by the journalist, particularly in the interviews that give him the basic material for his story.

These "honest serving men" are also of great value for the attention-giver who can focus attention on his attention-receiver by inviting him to present his ideas on a given subject. Examples are:

> How do you think society should go about handling this problem?
>
> What have you been doing about this difficulty?
>
> Why should we examine this matter?
>
> Tell me how the attitudes of these people affect others.
>
> Where is the best place for us to start?
>
> Who is the best person to take charge of this enterprise?

The subject is on stage, with all attention on his important views on a variety of subjects.

If you are going to use the question as a part of your attention-giving armament you must beware of the temptation to think you are conducting a cross-examination. Forget the court scenes in movie "who 'dun' its."

One year it was my privilege to visit Pelican Island on the Indian River in Florida. It was a tremendous experience. We boarded an air boat, skimmed along in inches of water, and saw the island covered with pelicans rising in a noisy, flapping cloud at our approach. Guided by the game warden, we peeked at nests and had eyeball contact with babies as big as eagles. We marveled at the ecological wonder of the cycle of fish providing food for pelicans, who in turn, fertilized the surrounding waters, causing the multiplication of marine life.

Ruth should be told about this. She is a member of the Audubon Society, an avid birder. As I thought of her, I mentally resolved that she would be the first person I'd contact when I arrived home.

Scarcely recovered from the trip, I picked up the phone and dialed Ruth's number.

"Ruth, this is John," I said.

"Hi, John," Ruth replied.

"Ruth, I had a wonderful experience. While I was in Florida I took a trip in an air boat to Pelican Island and saw the one place in the U.S. where pelicans nest and breed in greater numbers," I explained.

"Were they white pelicans or brown pelicans?" she asked.

"I don't know," I answered.

"You don't know! Didn't the ranger explain the difference types and colors?" she asked.

"Well, no, they all looked sort of dirty," I told her.

"The white pelican has a wing span of about nine feet, the brown only six feet. The white pelican flies with its head kind of hunched back. If it plunges into the water when seeking its food, it would be a brown pelican. On the other hand, if it were a white pelican, it would scoop up fish while it was swimming. Does that help you John?" she asked.

"Er . . . yes. Oh, Ruth, there is someone at the door. Why don't I call you back later?" I inquired.

Ruth's cross-examination had demoralized me. I had called with the hope that I might be an *attention-receiver*, but she wouldn't let me, she tried to turn me into an *attention-giver*.

There is all the difference in the world between a district attorney fighting to get the truth out of a reticent criminal, and an attention-giver trying to give his subject some positive-focused attention. If you are going to be successful, you must fight back every urge you have to cross examine your subject.

The Importance of the Now

The late President Kennedy was widely known for his witty answers to questions at his news conferences. It is not such common knowledge that he had a peculiar ability to ask an incisive question and pay unusual attention to what was said in reply. Robert Saudek conferred with the President while producing the television series, *Profiles in Courage,* and reported,

> He made you think he had nothing else to do except ask you questions and listen—with extraordinary concentration—to your answers. You knew that for the time being he had blotted out both the past and the future. More than anyone else I have ever met, President Kennedy seemed to understand the importance of the now.

"The importance of the now" is a phrase that conveys the skill of the *attention-giver*. The *attention-receiver* becomes aware that this is his special moment.

The Opening Question

The attention-giver can open a conversation with a question. However, he must remember that he is not seeking facts but is trying to focus on his subject, his emotional reactions, his opinions, and his ideas. One simple rule of thumb is: Never ask a question that can be answered with *yes* or *no*, unless you have a follow-up query.

You are talking with Joe Jones, who you know is depressed about his family situation, and who you feel needs some positive attention. One way to deal with the situation would be to ask him, "Do you like living with your brother?" The obvious answer would be either *yes* or *no*, and after one or the other has been verbalized, be uncertain as to what to say next.

The better response would be, "How do you feel about living with your brother?" This form of question will hopefully give him a sense of your interest and provide him with an opportunity to express the pent-up emotions.

Try your skill with attention-giving questions. Some of them are good and some of them are poor. Make your choice and indicate *G* for good and *B* for bad.

(1) Did you have a good day? ( )
(2) How do you feel about this? ( )
(3) Do you like your work? ( )
(4) Have you any ideas on the subject? ( )
(5) Oh, really? ( )
(6) Would you explain this to me? ( )
(7) Will you accept this new offer? ( )
(8) What is your reaction? ( )
(9) Do you love me? ( )
(10) Please give me your opinion ( )

Questions 1, 3, 5, 7, and 9 are poor, because they can be answered with *yes* or *no*. Questions 2, 4, 6, 8, and 10 are better, because they give the respondent attention by allowing him to express his feelings.

The following are some guidelines for effective attention-giving questions:

• Ask your question—then keep quiet so he can express himself.

- Ask questions that come closest to the other person's interest and will get the best answers.
- Be prepared to wait for the answer; don't be frightened of a period of silence.
- In every instance, the quality of the answer will reveal the quality of the question—try to plan it carefully.
- Questions that deal with the feelings are more provocative than those dealing with facts.

Managing the Flow

One observer of the attention processes has drawn an analogy from the field of economics. Like the competition in economics where a businessman tries to overcome his competitors, in conversation an individual tries to dominate the situation as the attention-getter. Derber[1] calls this conversational narcissism which interrupts the conversational flow.

The question enters into the arena here. There are two types of attention responses. Derber calls these the *shift response* and the *support response*. Examples of these would be:

> *Harry*: I saw Dan yesterday at the meeting.
> *Bill*: I haven't seen him in a long time. (shift response)
> *Harry*: I saw Dan yesterday at the meeting.
> *Bill*: How's he doing these days? (support response)

Derber claims both the shift response and the support response are like a commodity that is used in the interchange. In the first interchange, the flow of attention Bill turns to himself, whereas in the second episode, Bill encourages Harry to continue and has kept the attention focused on him.

If the premise of this authority is correct and attention is an interactional currency the question will be of primary importance. "Behold the Wicked Little Barb,/ Which catches fish in human garb."

Note

1. Charles Derber, *The Pursuit of Attention* (New York: Oxford University Press, 1979), 23.

12

Using the Magic of Touch

*"Some of the most crucial functions of the body
are only skin deep"*
—*Rosenfeld*

One woman who helped other women to improve their appearance with make-up, Estee Lauder, surely learned the importance of touch. She said,

> I touched, I touched, I never stopped touching. When I was building a business, I reached out and touched strangers in an elevator as I suggested they try a little of my cream blush. My father was from the old school. 'Estee—all that touching,' he used to say. He hated it. Thought it was for peasants. But, what I liked to do better than anything else in the world was to touch faces. I have never stopped.

This touching paid off as she went on to become the make-up tycoon of the world.

Estee Lauder's success with make-up reminds us of the importance of the skin of which it is said, "The skin is a convuluted body sock which we wear."[1] Its function is vital in a strange way, "Our image of the human body is largely defined by what we see in the mirror, what we can touch with our hands, not heart or brain, not lung or liver, not even muscle or bone—but our skin."[2]

Healing of the Body

The touch has long been associated with healing, and the Bible tells of many healings which took place by means of a touch. "And Jesus put forth his hand, and touched him [the leper], saying, I will; be thou clean. And immediately his leprosy was cleansed" (Matt. 8:3). The Bible says about Peter's mother-in-law, "And he touched her hand, and the fever left her: and she arose, and ministered unto them" (Matt. 8:15). It says about the blind men, "So Jesus had compassion on them, and touched their eyes: and immediately their eyes received sight, and they followed him" (Matt. 20:34). Jesus' treatment of the deaf man with an impediment in his speech was described in the Bible: "He took him aside from the multitude, and put his fingers into his ears, and he spit, and touched his tongue" (Mark 7:33). The high priest's servant's ear was severed by "one of them [who] smote the servant of the high priest, and cut off his right ear. And Jesus answered and said, Suffer ye thus far. And he touched his ear, and healed him" (Luke 22:50-51).

The apostle Paul's ministry involved a continued use of the touch in healing. An example would be with Publius's father, "And it came to pass, that the father of Publius lay sick of a fever and of a bloody flux: to whom Paul entered in, and prayed, and laid his hands on him, and healed him" (Acts 28:8).

In England, it used to be that the king's touch had healing powers. It started with Edward the Confessor. Sick people kneeled before the king who touched them, while his chaplain intoned, "He put his hands upon them and healed them." Queen Anne was the last of the British rulers to practice the "king's touch." The practice spread to the continent, but not all rulers were convinced. William of Orange considered the practice a mere superstition and only touched one person. During the process he muttered, "May God give you better health and more sense."

In more recent days has come an enormous interest in healing techniques utilizing touch. One recent book on the subject has listed some of the methods as Therapeutic Touch, Acupuncture, Acupressure, Chinese Massage, Shiatsu, Reiki, Polarity Therapy, Reichian Massage, Bioenergetics, Rolfing, Alexander Technique, Feldenkrais, Osteopathy, Chiropractric, Applied Kinesiology, Touch for Health, Swedish Massage, and Reflexology. All of these utilize some form of touch technique.

One of the explanations which seems to underlie most of the touch therapies is stated by an investigator, ". . . a human being's energy extends slightly beyond what we perceive as his boundary—the skin—and he is interconnected through this energy with everything in his environment. If this is so, the energy within the body can be influenced . . . by manipulating energy fields outside and immediately adjacent to the body."[3]

As a boy in my native Australia, I frequently joined with a group of my friends in a simple, pleasurable activity. We periodically visited an amusement park attracted by an unusual machine. Forming a human chain, the boy at one end holding the handle, the youth at the other end of the chain slowly turned the crank. With that turning, a current of electricity flowed through the human chain to many delighted squeals and warnings that no one must break contact.

Ashley Montague reminds us that even without a generating machine there is an electrical discharge from the skin, and many people report that when they touch or are touched they have a feeling of "a sort of electrical current" passing through them. The skin is a good electrical conductor and the electric discharges from the skin can actually be measured with instruments. The best known of which is the spychogalvanometer, as Montague says, "commonly miscalled the lie detector." He also notes that emotional changes within the individual lead to an increase in the electrical conductance of the skin across the palms and hands and feet.[4]

The movement of electrical current gives us an illustration of the reason why touching is so effective as a means of conveying and receiving attention as it passes from one individual to another. There are two types of electrical current—*direct*, generally written DC, which indicates that electrons are moving in one direction from positive to negative, and the other type is *alternating*, written AC, in which the current constantly changes direction with the electrons moving forward and backward. Touching is an AC experience. I touch and am touched. "Touching is the only sense that relies on cooperation. You can't give a touch without getting one right back. You can talk, listen, smell, and taste alone but touching is a reciprocal act,"[5] which is one of the reasons why touching is so important as an instrument in expressive attention.

The Largest Organ of the Body

The skin is the largest organ of the body and is sometimes called the "mother of the senses." Like some tremendous garment, it is in a constant state of renewing itself; skin cells are shed at the rate of more than a million an hour, and about every four hours or so, it forms two new layers of cells. "The epidermis is constantly regenerating itself; all its cells turn themselves over every twenty eight days or so. Dead cells are being steadily sloughed as new ones push."[6]

This skin can be thought of in two ways. As is seen in the word *psychosomatic*, the mind from within expresses itself through skin. The other way is for the skin to receive messages from the outside world and tell what is going on around us. "The bottle that contains us has to be porous, and at the same time reliably leakproof, awash as we are in vital fluids that never hold still."[7]

The importance of the skin is seen in the skin terms that have become a part of our language. We speak of people who are insensitive as being "callous" or "prickly," and of some we say they are "thin-skinned" or "thick-skinned." We know of people who "get under our skin" and others have a shallowness which leads us to describe them as only "skin deep."

However, it is the word *touch* that the use of skin terms really takes off. People are said to "rub us the wrong way." The skill of relating to people involves "the personal touch." Someone who does well has a "magic touch." Over-sensitive people are "touchy."

Few of us realize the importance of touch as a factor in life. I once knew a man who cut his arm requiring stitches, but when the doctor closed the wound, he neglected to take care of a severed nerve. When the wound healed he had no sensitivity in the outer edge of his hand and while working as a cabinetmaker badly tore up the skin because of his lack of feeling. Without tactile senses we are in trouble.

One investigator said it well, "The greatest sense of our body is our touch sense. It is probably the chief sense in the processes of sleeping and waking; it gives us knowledge of depth or thickness and form; we feel, we love and hate, are touchy and are touched through the touch corpuscles of the skin."[8]

When Martin Luther was summoned to appear before the Diet of Worms, the lowly monk was apprehensive and concerned. However, as he walked into the bishop's palace, he, standing before Charles V, the emperor of the Holy Roman Empire, had a certain confident air about him. A contemporary noted, "The fool entered smiling."

To understand what had happened, we look into the courtyard outside the palace. As Luther pushed his way through the crowd, General Frundsberg, the most illustrious soldier in Germany at that time, said to him, "Be of good courage; God will not forsake thee." As he spoke the encouraging words, the rough soldier reached out and put his arm around Luther's shoulder. That gesture, that touch, might have been even more important than the words the General spoke and, at least in part, accounted for the energetic manner in which Luther entered the building.[9]

From Birth to Old Age

The British House of Commons is sometimes called the "Mother of Parliaments" and has produced some of the all-important statements upon which the development of democracy has taken place. From this august institution came a paper reflecting the work of a parliamentary committee on the problem of battered children. The committee reported that annually about 300 children are killed by their parents, and over a thousand under four years of age are severely injured. The major recommendation of the paper was a major preventative step which would be for the mother to kiss and cuddle her newborn baby, thus providing skin bonding between mother and child.

Great numbers of studies have been carried out showing the importance of a mother and her newborn baby having some type of physical contact. Commenting on the work of Harlow with monkeys, in which he demonstrated the importance of bodily contact of mother and child, one investigator noted, "As they learn to touch they learn to love." This contact starts the all-important bonding process for both mother and child, but it does not end here. The human needs touching experiences all one's days.

In one's initial experiences of life, the baby has her most pleasurable skin experiences through her lips as she sucks at the formula bottle or her mother's breast, and these will continue to be an avenue of pleasure for the rest of her days and will later give rise to the experience of kissing. Kissing is one of the prime examples of giving attention by touch. It is one of the uniquely human behaviors—no animals kiss. Even among humans there is a divergence. The Japanese did not have a word for kiss, and some natives in the South Sea islands prefer by far to rub noses.

It has been said that a kiss is a contraction of the lips that comes from an expansion of the heart, but it can have different motivations which are indicated by the way it is performed, such as the child's appearance of a willingness to endure the experience, the maiden lady's prim peck, the expansive aunt's slobber, the lover's protracted contact, or in modern soap opera practice which gives the impression that the two participants have returned to cannibalism and are trying to eat each other.

The Bible speaks of kissing, but it may not be the lip kissing rather a kissing of the hand, forehead, or cheek, still a significant skin contact. The New Testament instructions are given to "Salute one another with an holy kiss" (Rom. 16:16), "greet ye one another with an holy kiss" (1 Cor. 16:28), "greet ye one another with a kiss of love" (1 Pet. 5:14, NIV). But with this as also with so many other life experiences, kisses have other possibilities, as when Joab as he kissed Amasa stabbed him with a knife (2 Sam. 20:9-10) or a Judas in the New Testament betrayed Jesus with a kiss (Luke 22:48).

Touching experiences may be even more important in old age. One poem poignantly states the situation:

How long has it been since someone touched me?
Twenty years?
Twenty years I've been a widow,
Respected.
Smiled at.
But never touched.
Never held so close that loneliness
was blotted out.[10]

The anthropologist Ashley Montague says hugs are of equal importance for the male. In old age, the male's sexual capacity is diminished. This means that "tactile hunger is more powerful than ever because it is the only sensuous experience that remains open to him." In this situation he is dependent more and more on friends and family and needs to be touched and hugged.

To Hug or Not to Hug

The mention of touching raises the issue of the practice of hugging and its rights and wrongs. A reader of a column in a religious newspaper wrote the following letter:

Dear John,
I read a recent reply of yours in which you said you approved of hugging. Let me tell you my experience.
A man from our church took to dropping in while my husband was at work. He hugged me, and I said we had better watch out that it didn't go any further. He laughed and said it was OK for Christians, so I went along with him until one day he really showed me that he had sexual experiences in mind. After quite a struggle, I made it clear to him that I thought it would be better that he not come around anymore. Do you still think hugging is OK?

Disturbed

The answer to this letter telling of such a lamentable experience is that there are certain criteria of hugging contained in the following statement which incorporates the concept of the "four wrongs" of hugging.

The problems of hugging come from hugging the wrong

person at the wrong time for the wrong reason with the wrong kind of hug.

The wrong person.—One psychologist has suggested that there are five categories of people who should be the subjects of touching experiences. The five categories of people are:

• *Functional-Professional* in which the toucher is such a person as a dress-maker, doctor, or barber. The touching is a part of the service being rendered and purely professional with no personal meaning.

• *Social-Polite* touches which are generally given to business associates or acquaintances. It may take the form of a handshake—friendly rather than intimate.

• *Friendship-Warmth* touching that takes place with friendly neighbors, people with whom we work, and extended family members. This is in between warmth and deep affection.

• *Love-Affection* touching experiences are between close family members. They may also include close friends.

• *Close-Intimacy* touching between husband and wife in the privacy of their own homes.[11]

The Friendship-Warmth would be the type with the greatest potential, but we must remember that another consideration would be the receiver of the contact. It is easy to hug a firm-fleshed child or an attractive young woman, but the people who need hugging most are the elderly and the unattractive. The exercise of friendship-warmth requires discipline and effort, but it can be highly effective.

The wrong time.—Is the hug furtive and shamefaced in some secluded spot? Or is it in the open in the view of all?

The wrong reason.—Does the "hugger" or "huggee" for that matter have in mind to exploit the other person? A viable hug is nondemanding.

The wrong kind of hug.—There are many different types of hugs as will be seen in the next section.

The Varieties of a Hug Experience

Not all hugs are of equal value. Some of the various types are:

The "Hi" hug.—This is a cursory slipping of the arms around each other and is a form of greeting.

The side-by-side hug.—The participants are standing and looking is the same direction, each one with an arm around each other's shoulder.

Let's-get-it-over hug.—This generally takes place when a child, probably at the behest of a parent, runs over turning the side of the face and hugging in the briefest period of time imaginable.

Who's-next? hug.—While this person is hugging, she is murmuring "sweet nothings" and looking on to the next prospective hugger.

Yellow rock.—A practice among square dancers in which the caller announces "Yellow Rock," and the participant turns and hugs the person on the left with an exclamation of joy.

The bone-crusher hug.—Seen in the famous Russian bear hug. If there is an unfortunate outcome, it will be the possibility of broken ribs.

A-frame hug.—Heads are politely making contact while legs and feet are as far apart as possible; the participants make a reversed *V*—a rather strange sight.

The warm, cuddly hug.—This is the therapeutic move that is easy to give and great to receive.

The consoling hug.—A gentle enfolding of a person who has just been hurt either physically or emotionally and is akin to a mother taking a child in her arms.

The exploitive hug.—The initiator of this experience has the hopes of causing the hugee to lose control and become willing to be submissive to the hugger's desires.

All the evidence shows that hugging is an important part of the enriching experiences of life. It may be one of the prime mechanisms by which love is conveyed and energy transferred from one person to another.

Hugs

It's wondrous what a hug can do.
A hug can cheer you when you're blue.
A hug can say, "I love you so,"
Or, "Gee, I hate to see you go."
A hug is, "Welcome back again,"
And "Great to see you! Where've you been?"
A hug can soothe a small child's pain
And bring a rainbow after rain.
The hug! There's no doubt about it—
We scarcely could survive without it!
A hug delights and warms and charms.
It must be why God gave us arms.
Hugs are great for fathers and mothers.
Sweet for sisters, swell for brothers.
And chances are your favorite aunts
Love them more than potted plants.
Kittens crave them. Puppies love them.
Heads of state are not above them.
A hug can break the language barrier
And make your travels so much merrier.
No need to fret about your store of 'em.
The more you give the more there's more of 'em.
So stretch those arms without delay
And *give someone a hug today*!!!

Touch has another important role in the realm of the spirit. It is used in designating spiritual leaders. The new leader of Israel was appointed, "And Joshua the son of Nun was full of the spirit of wisdom; for Moses had laid his hands upon him" (Deut. 34:9). When Paul and Barnabas were set apart to go on a new missionary enterprise, touch was involved. "And when they had fasted and prayed, and laid their hands on them, they sent them away" (Acts 13:3). The choice of new deacons in the young church resulted in the selection of seven men, and "Whom they set before the apostles: and when they had prayed, they laid their hands on them" (Acts 6:6).

This is the touch par excellence.

Notes

1. Albert Rosenfeld, "Some of the body's most crucial functions are only skin deep," *Smithsonian*, May 1988, 159.

2. Ibid.

3. Sherry Suib Cohen, *The Magic of Touch* (New York: Harper & Row, 1987), 64.

4. Ashley Montague, *Touching: The Human Significance of Skin* (New York: Harper and Row, 1986), 62.

5. Cohen, 10.

6. Rosenfeld, 159.

7. Ibid.

8. J. Lionel Taylor, *The Stages of Human Life,* 157.

9. Thomas M. Lindsay, *A History of the Reformation*, (Edinburgh: T & T Clark, 1959), 279.

10. Donna Swansson, "Minnie Remembers" quoted in Montague, 397.

11. Richard Heslin, quoted in Steven Thayer, "Close Encounters," *Psychology Today*, March 1988, 31.

13

Using the Power of Praise

"[Tribute comes from her husband, he says,]
There are many fine women in the world,
but you are the best of them all! "
(Prov. 31:29, TLB).

What is the purpose of marriage? There have been many attempts to answer this question—companionship, sexual fulfillment, or producing a family. None of these— if we are to believe a New England maker of apple cider. Looking back over fifty years of married life he said, "I reckon the best marriages are really mutual admiration societies. My wife likes a little compliment from time to time and so do I."

These words of wisdom remind us of the New Testament where there is a warning to husbands and wives that tells us "Defraud ye not one the other" (1 Cor. 7:5). In its context, of course, it refers to sexual obligation, but it can just as easily be applied to using praise for each other in marriage.

One of the objections sometimes raised to this concept is, "Are you telling me to flatter my wife?" The answer is that flattery *is* fraud, but we should also remember that when we withhold deserved praise it is a form of cheating in marriage.

The Awesome Power of Praise

This excursion into the arena of marriage reminds us that the highest form of attention is praise. The dictionary defines this word, "An expression of warm approval, admiration, or commendation . . ." To use this form of attention effectively, you will have to learn some skills. These will include:

Look for something to praise rather than criticize.—Our little dog had grown old but not very gracefully. At one stage in his life, he had been involved in a fight from which he emerged with one eye rather badly damaged. As a result, this damaged eye had a bad habit of turning in the wrong direction and showing a white area which gave him a peculiar, somewhat sinister appearance at times.

The passing years had also brought on an arthritic condition that settled in his left rear leg. As it became more painful, the little dog gave up using the sore limb and made a rather pathetic picture as he limped along on three legs. Because he found handling so painful, we had given up on having him clipped or combing his coat. A French poodle with long, unkept hair does not present a very attractive sight.

Ginger Hazelton, an eleven-year-old, was visiting our home. She was on her best behavior and hard at work commending everything in our house, and when she faced the poodle, her capacity to commend met its supreme test.

There stood the poodle, one leg painfully drawn under him, an eye that made him look like a canine Peter Lorre, and his matted hair giving him the appearance of a dried-out mop. Ginger's attention to detail provided her with the opening she needed as she commented, "He sure knows how to wag his tail."

Look for Something to Praise Rather than Criticize

It may take you some time, but if you look long enough, you will find something to compliment. In this way you will be able to help a fellow human do something about developing his or her potential.

Make your praise descriptive.—Some enthusiast reading about the potency of praise is likely to say, "Well, if running around flattering people is all I have to do, I can easily manage that," and launches himself on a program of pouring out syrupy compliments commending mediocrity and winning his way with flattery. While this line of approach may go over with some people for a short time, there's a good chance that in the long run a good proportion of people will see through him, and he will antagonize many of his subjects.

Practitioners of these techniques of saccharin and syrup overlook the factor of satiation. Experience has shown that almost any appetite can be satiated. With this factor in mind, we must not praise indiscriminately but will make praise descriptive.

Dr. Sam Harrison is a remarkably successful neurosurgeon with a talented wife and a bevy of beautiful daughters. This medico has not only maintained his professional competence but has developed remarkable relationship skills which have made him enormously popular with the staffs of the hospitals where he works. When his name is mentioned during the bridge game, the women "oohh" and "aahh" murmuring such phrases as, "Isn't he a doll?" "I just adore that man," and "I think he is a darling."

Many of them recall stories of friends, acquaintances, and relatives who have been saved from death by this doctor's diagnostic and surgical skills. However, it is his tech-

niques of relating that have raised the level of popularity
of this medico. He has an unusual capacity to commend
people. Once again, as in so many things he undertakes,
he adopts a unique way of doing this.

While examining X-rays, he turns to the technician
and says, "These certainly are wonderful pictures. You
really know how to get the exact position I need." Looking
at a patient swathed in bandages he tells the nurse, "If an
Egyptian Pharaoh had ever heard about you, he certainly
would have employed you as a bandager of the royal
mummies." Sitting for long hours watching his neigh-
bor's slides and the interminable commentary he remarks, "That picture from the Star Ferry shows the way
in which a good shot can be framed and made so much
more attractive."One friend of Dr. Harrison remarked,
"Sam would have a good word to say about the devil."

Learn from Dr. Harrison; *Particularize your praise.*
Don't just say, "You're a good boy," but "You did a wonderful job on the lawn." Not "Good meal, Honey," but
"That was wonderful the way you served the broccoli and
carrots, it certainly had eye appeal."

Praise is multiplied by the number of people hearing.—
One wife in a confrontation with her husband about his
criticism of her said, "The very worst aspect of that rebuke was that you did it in public. Never, never, never
correct me in the presence of others!" Turn this around
and it will mean that the effectiveness of a compliment is
multiplied by the number of people present.

It is of interest to notice how the Bible uses the princi-
ple of descriptive and public praise. In the Old Testament,
the statement of the Lord to Jehu is, "Because thou hast
done well in executing that which is right in mine eyes,
and hast done unto the house of Ahab according to all
that was in mine heart, thy children of the fourth generation shall sit on the throne of Israel" (2 Kings 10:30).

In the ministry of Jesus, we see the way He praises the committed servant, "His lord said unto him, Well done, thou good and faithful servant: thou hast been faithful over a few things, I will make thee ruler over many things: enter thou into the joy of thy lord" (Matt. 25:21).

When Jesus heard the statement of the centurion that it was not necessary for him to come to the soldier's house but only to speak the word for his servant to be healed, "he marvelled, *and said to them that followed,* Verily I say unto you, I have not found so great faith, no, not in Israel" (Matt. 8:10, author's italics). Here is an example of the descriptive-public technique of effective praising. *The size of the audience multiplies the effect of praise for individuals.*

Have some praise statements in mind.—It might well be that praise statements do not come readily to mind when you need them. Unless you have a very good vocabulary, there's a chance that you won't find it easy to come up with the right word at the right time. To help in this you should write a list of statements you can use. The following are some words or phrases that a person could use with children:

Good	Thank you
That's right	I'm pleased with that
Excellent	Great
That's clever	Groovy
Exactly	I like that
Good job	I love you
Good thinking	That's interesting
That shows a great deal of work	That's smart
You really pay attention	That was very kind of you
You should show this to your father	
Show Grandma your picture	

Look over the situation in which you are working. Examine the person you are trying to influence. Check him or her out. Find out some of the things about her that you can commend at the appropriate time. Prepare some statements and have them ready to use at the best time.

Work on upgrading your praise quotient.—You might have an idea from Sydney Webb who is a supervisor with the Carnation Paper Cup Company. He realized that while he comes down heavily on any employee who makes a mistake, he seldom has praise for anybody. After attending a motivational workshop on The Praise Factor, he decided to give it a shot and set up a program to follow in praising others.

Webb uses his diary as means of developing his "praise quotient." In one corner of each daily segment of his date book, he puts PR or praise section. Each day he enters his score with the aim of making and recording the number of praise statements he makes each day. His goal is to make ten praise statements a day. Hopefully, he will establish a praise habit that will improve his personality and his relationship skills.

In his story of Gulliver's stay in Lilliput, Swift tells of his discovery of a peculiarity of their legal system. When Gulliver told the Lilliputians about the English system of justice which punished lawbreakers, they were astonished. They told him the shortcoming of the English system was the neglect of rewards. The Lilliputians placed a statue representing justice on the top of their Courts of Judicature. The statue had six eyes, two looking ahead, two looking backward, and one on each side of the head. Justice held in her right hand a bag of gold and in her left a sheathed sword with the intent of revealing, in Gulliver's words, "To show she is more disposed to reward than to punish."

Like that statue of justice, we must learn to look in all directions, overlooking some things but constantly alert for the opportunities to use praise power. As we will see in the next chapter, praise is so important that even God demands it from His people.

14

Paying Attention to God

*"If only you had paid attention to my commands,
your peace would have been like a river,
your righteousness like the waves of the sea"*
(Isa. 48:18, NIV).

The story of Samuel is a study in attention. It began with Hannah, the childless wife of Elkanah, for whom the word *barren* cut like a lash. In her dilemma she spent time seeking God's attention imploring Him for the blessing of motherhood. Eli, the priest, came to her in the tabernacle, and having heard her story, assured her that her request for a child would be granted, and she, certain that God had given her His attention, was delighted when she gave birth to a son. Hannah's son was named Samuel, which indicated she had been paying attention to God, and Him to her, because it meant, "asked of the Lord."

This was a unique period in Israel's history of which it was said, "There were very few messages from the Lord and visions from him were quite rare" (1 Sam. 3:1, GNB). The reason for this situation was that Israel was ignoring God and not paying attention to Him.

The breakthrough came when the boy, living in the tabernacle with Eli, the aged priest, thought he heard Eli summoning him. As every Sunday School child knows, on the third occasion came the voice, "Samuel, Samuel," and

Samuel indicated to God that he was paying attention, "Speak; for thy servant heareth" (1 Sam.3:10).

This story may be a parable telling us that the God who created the world wants to communicate with His world, but few people are giving Him their attention, and the message is unheard.

Does God Need Human Attention?

There is much in the Bible that would indicate God has strong desire to have the attention of His people. After Adam's transgression, God called for his attention, "Where art thou?" In the Book of Job, where Job is pondering life and the mystery of suffering, there are at least two occasions when God calls for consideration of another factor in the equation, "But now, Job, listen to my words, pay attention to everything I say" (Job 33:1). "Pay attention, Job, and listen to me, be silent and I will speak" (v. 31, NIV).

Recalling the use of the metaphor of attention starvation used in the first chapter of this book, there comes the promise of what God will do for those who give Him attention, "Ho, every one that thirsteth, come ye to the waters, and he that hath no money; come ye, buy, and eat; yea, come, buy wine and milk without money and without price" (Isa. 55:1).

The Loving Eye of the Mind

John Wesley, a master of the spiritual life, painted a picture of the type of attention which believers should give to their God,

> . . . his heart is ever lifted up to, at all times in all places. In this time he is never hindered, much less interrupted by any person or thing. In retirement or company, in leisure, business, or conversation, his heart is ever with the Lord. Whether he lie down or rise up, God is in all his thoughts; he walks with God contin-

ually, having the loving eye of his mind still fixed upon him, and everywhere "seeing Him that is invisible."[1]

There are few spiritual giants who live up to this standard, and there were many periods of dissension among God's people which gave rise to the frequently quoted statement about the way to a fulfilling spiritual experience, "If my people, which are called by my name, shall humble themselves, and pray, and seek my face, and turn from their wicked ways; then will I hear from heaven, and will forgive their sin, and will heal their land" (2 Chron. 7:14). The gist of this statement is obviously the demand of God that His people will be serious about their relationship with Him and show this frame of mind by paying special attention to Him.

In reviewing the accounts of times of spiritual revival, there are many records of seasons of prayer and confession in which the supplicants paid much attention to God by offering their petitions to Him and seeking to change their life-style so He would see that they were noting His requirements of holy living.

The New Testament contains a statement of Jesus concerning the failure of the people to pay attention to John the Baptist or His message;

> But whereunto shall I liken this generation? It is like unto children sitting in the markets, and calling unto their fellows, And saying, We have piped unto you, and ye have not danced; we have mourned unto you, and ye have not lamented. For John came neither eating nor drinking, and they say, He hath a devil. The Son of man came eating and drinking, and they say, Behold a man gluttonous, and a winebibber, a friend of publicans and sinners. But wisdom is justified of her children (Matt. 11:16).

The accusation of Jesus—this generation, no matter how they are approached, will not pay attention.

Similarly, in the most telling frustration of all concerning people who would not pay attention to His message,

Jesus made one of His most poignant statements: "O Jerusalem, Jerusalem, thou that killest the prophets, and stonest them which are sent unto thee, how often would I have gathered thy children together, even as a hen gathereth her chickens under her wings, and ye would not! Behold, your house is left unto you desolate" (Matt. 23:37-38).

We have already, in a series of earlier chapters, examined the levels of attention, looking, listening, concerned questioning, touching, and praising. In this concluding chapter, we will consider each of these levels of attention and note what God says in respect to them in the Bible.

Level-One Attention: Looking

The desire of God that people should look to Him is mentioned a number of times in both the Old and the New testaments. The beginning of a religious experience comes with a look: "*Look unto me*, and be ye saved, all the ends of the earth: for I am God, and there is none else" (Isa. 45:22, author's italics). And as the believer anticipates his future, he realizes he will continue to keep his eyes in the proper direction. "At that day shall a man look to his Maker, and his eyes shall have respect to the Holy One of Israel" (Isa. 17:7). In his devotional life, the believer must keep his attention in the right direction, "Therefore I will *look unto the Lord*; I will wait for the God of my salvation: my God will hear me" (Mic. 7:7, author's italics). The early-morning hour becomes significant: "My voice shalt thou hear in the morning, O Lord; in the morning will I direct my prayer unto thee, and will *look up*" (Ps. 5:3, author's italics). When he feels that he may have been alienated from God, he will continue to look. "Then I said, I am cast out of thy sight; yet *I will look again* toward thy holy temple" (Jon. 2:4, author's italics).

The clarion voice of the prophet Zechariah anticipated the coming of the Messiah, His humiliation, and the ultimate realization of His mission,

> And I will pour upon the house of David, and upon the inhabitants of Jerusalem, the spirit of grace and of supplications: and *they shall look upon me* whom they have pierced, and they shall mourn for him, as one mourneth for his only son, and shall be in bitterness for him, as one that is in bitterness for his firstborn (Zech. 12:10, author's italics).

The Heavenly Sacrifice has been made and the promise of the second coming is given unto those who are paying attention, "So Christ was once offered to bear the sins of many; and *unto them that look for him* shall he appear the second time without sin unto salvation" (Heb. 9:28, author's italics). This experience has set the pattern for the believer's posture, "*Looking unto Jesus* the author and finisher of our faith; who for the joy that was set before him endured the cross, despising the shame, and is set down at the right hand of the throne of God" (Heb. 12:2, author's italics).

The importance of placing the attention in the right direction is emphasized in reference to the Old Testament concerning Lot's wife as Jesus declared as follows, "Remember Lot's wife"(Luke 17:32), and sent His hearer's minds back to the incident, "But his wife *looked back* from behind him, and she became a pillar of salt" (Gen. 19:26).

Level-One Attention is an important part of the Christian life as we seek to respond to God's desire for attention from His children.

Level-Two Attention: Listening

The prime statement of Judaism's faith is the Shema, "*Hear* O Israel, the Lord our God is one Lord" (Deut. 6:4, author's italics) which by its very name emphasizes the importance that God places on attention. The word *hear* is used 516 times in the *King James Version* of the Bible, and in the New Testament as in the Old, Jesus made a similar emphasis: "And Jesus answered him, The first of all the commandments is, *Hear*, O Israel; The Lord our God is one Lord" (Mark 12:29, author's italics). "He that hath ears to hear, *let him hear*" (Matt. 11:15, author's italics), and almost in exasperation Jesus says, ". . . having ears, hear ye not?" (Mark 8:18).

God's people must give Him their attention and the most widely recognized means of doing this is to listen for the voice of the Master.

Level-Three Attention: Concerned Questioning

The best example of concerned questioning as a means of paying attention to God will be prayer.

"And Abram said, Lord God, what wilt thou give me?" (Gen. 15:2). "David said, Who am I, O Lord God?" (2 Sam. 7:18). Cornelius said, "What is it, Lord?" (Acts 10:4). The people lifted up their voices, "and said, O Lord God of Israel, why is this come to pass in Israel?" (Judg. 21:3). "I will say unto God my rock, Why hast thou forgotten me? why go I mourning because of the oppression of the enemy?" (Ps. 42:9).

The most personal and intimate of all the indicators of humankind's relationship with God is seen in each individual's prayer life. The promises of the blessings that can come to an individual are limitless, and "More things are wrought by prayer Than this world dreams of" (Tennyson). Despite all this, prayer might well be the most neglected of all the spiritual disciplines.

Possibly the most well-known and frequently practiced use of prayer to gain God's attention is in connection with illness:

Is any among you afflicted? let him pray. Is any merry? let him sing psalms. Is any sick among you? let him call for the elders of the church; and let them pray over him, anointing him with oil in the name of the Lord: And the prayer of faith shall save the sick, and the Lord shall raise him up; and if he have committed sins, they shall be forgiven him. Confess your faults one to another, and pray one for another, that ye may be healed. The effectual fervent prayer of a righteous man availeth much." (Jas. 5:13-16).

According to this passage God is not burdened but rather delighted when His people give Him attention by bringing their prayer requests to Him.

Jesus wanted the attention of His disciples and said, "Watch with me" as He faced the ever-present problem of maintaining His disciples's attention. From the larger group Jesus had selected the inner circle of Peter, James, and John in the garden of Gethsemane and taken them to accompany Him as He moved to the more intimate relationship with His Father.

Following His agonizing with His Heavenly Father about His impending experience, Jesus returned and found His disciples sleeping and rebuked them, "What, could ye not watch with me for one hour?" The experience was repeated twice more, and Jesus finally said in sorrowful resignation, "Sleep on now and take your rest"(Matt. 26:40-45).

Jesus wanted their attention, and He wants ours today. He continues to urge us to pray, and the heart of prayer is attention. Attention is the essence of prayer, and as soon as attention ceases—prayer ceases.

It might well be that, as the reader goes through this volume, there could be an unanticipated by-product. In learning the skills of getting and giving attention, there will always be the possibility of a new level of spiritual experience as attention is focused beyond ourselves and our fellow men and women to the *divine*.

Level-Four Attention: Touching

This level of attention, touching, does not seem to be applicable to a relationship with God who is spirit, and the idea of touching as a means of giving attention seems at first consideration to be rather ridiculous. However, when we remember the way that God revealed Himself to the world, we are better able to understand. "And without controversy great is the mystery of godliness: *God was manifest in the flesh*" (1 Tim. 3:16, author's italics). This manifestation took place in the Person of Jesus Christ, and it will be profitable for us to consider the second Person of the Godhead in our study of Divine attention.

In the ministry of Jesus, it seems as if He responded to people who gave Him their strength by touching. So it is recorded, "And whithersoever he entered, into villages, or cities, or country, they laid the sick in the streets, and besought him that they might *touch* if it were but the border of his garment: and as many *as touched him* were made whole" (Mark 6:56, author's italics). "And besought him that they might only *touch* the hem of his garment: and as many as *touched* were made perfectly whole" (Matt. 14:36, author's italics).

One case is highly individual, "When she had heard of Jesus, came in the press behind, and touched his garment. For she said, *If I may touch but his clothes*, I shall be whole. And straightway the fountain of her blood was dried up; and she felt in her body that she was healed of that plague" (Mark 5:27-29, author's italics).

And it could be that God wants attention from His people and may be wanting them to touch Him.

Level-Five Attention: Praising

At the highest level of attention, praising, we find the word praise or praising used some 226 times throughout the Bible. There is the specific statement from God, "Whoso offereth praise glorifieth me" (Ps. 50:23). In response came the words of the psalmist, "I will be glad and rejoice in thee: I will sing praise to thy name, O thou most High" (Ps. 9:2). "And my tongue shall speak of thy righteousness and of thy praise all the day long" (Ps. 35:28).

Music played a large part in the activities of praising God.

Praise the Lord with harp: sing unto him with the psaltery and an instrument of ten strings (33:2).

And he appointed certain of the Levites to minister before the ark of the Lord, and to record, and to thank and praise the Lord God of Israel (1 Chron. 16:4).

Moreover four thousand were porters; and four thousand praised the LORD with the instruments which I made, said David, to praise therewith (1 Chron. 23:5).

Jehoshaphat prepared his people for what must have been an imposing sight as his army marched on parade,

And when he had consulted with the people, he appointed singers unto the Lord, and that should praise the beauty of holiness, as they went out before the army, and to say, Praise the Lord; for his mercy endureth forever (2 Chron. 20:21).

Of Jeduthun: the sons of Jeduthun; Gedaliah, and Zeri, and Jeshaiah, Hashabiah, and Mattithiah, six, under the hands of their father Jeduthun, who prophesied with a harp, to give thanks and to praise the Lord (1 Chron. 25:3).

But preeminently praise is a personal experience. "And he hath put a new song in my mouth, even praise unto our God: many shall see it, and fear, and shall trust in the Lord" (Ps. 40:3). "O Lord, open thou my lips; and my mouth shall show forth thy praise" (51:15). "So will I sing praise unto thy name for ever, that I may daily perform my vows" (61:8).

Earlier in this volume we noted that there are different types of attention, *unfocused*, the type of generalized attention, "Let the heaven and earth praise him, the seas, and everything that moveth therein" (Ps.69:34); *partly focused*, in which attention is divided, ". . . for I had gone with the multitude, I went with them to the house of God, with the voice of joy and praise, with a multitude that kept holy day" (42:4); and *focused*, "Let my mouth be filled with thy praise and with thy honor all the day" 71:8). Praise is closely focused attention. This act of praise is particularly important, and in a number of places it is referred to as sacrifice. "By him therefore let us offer the sacrifice of praise to God continually, that is, the fruit of our lips giving thanks to his name" (Heb. 13:15).

Perhaps the most touching of all the cries of Deity for attention is seen the word of the prophet as he forecast the feelings of the Messiah in His moment of forsakenness: "Is it nothing to you, all ye that pass by? Behold and see if there be any sorrow like unto my sorrow, which is done unto me (Lam. 1:12).

At radio station KVIL in Dallas, Texas, an announcer, upset by the way that the populace was being exploited by pitchmen on radio and television who were constantly appealing for funds, decided to conduct an experiment of his own. He asked, without giving any reason for the appeal, that his listeners send him a check for $20. The response exceeded his wildest expectations as listeners mailed in $243,000 in $20 checks. The announcer's biggest problem was to decide what charity to which to donate the money.

What a vivid contrast this willingness to give makes with the scant attention we pay to the Savior who seeks our attention. G. Studdart-Kennedy, chaplain during

World War I and known to the troops as "Woodbine Willy," composed a poem in which he endeavored to reflect the situation of Jesus in his reaction to inattention.

Indifference

When Jesus came to Golgotha they hanged Him on a tree,
They drave great nails through hands and feet, and made
a Calvary;
They crowned Him with a crown of thorns, red were His
wounds and deep,
For those were crude and cruel days, and human flesh was
cheap.

When Jesus came to Birmingham, they simply passed Him
by,
They never hurt a hair of Him, they only let Him die:
For men had grown more tender, they would not give Him
pain,
They only just passed down the street, and left Him in the
rain.

Still Jesus cried, "Forgive them, for they know not what
they do,"
And still it rained the winter rain that drenched Him
through and through;
The crowds went home and left the streets without a soul
to see,
And Jesus crouched against a wall and cried for Calvary.

Inattentive humans might represent the ultimate punishment of our Lord by His creatures.

Join me in the prayer of the famous sculptor Michelangelo:

Do thou, then, breathe those thoughts into my mind
By which such virtue may be in me be bred
That in thy holy footsteps I may tread:
The fetters of my tongue do thou unbind,
That I may have the power to sing of thee
And sound thy praise everlastingly.

Note

1. *The Works of John Wesley* (Grand Rapids: The Zondervan Publishing House), vol. viii, 343.